£4   01/04

ROADWAYS

THE HISTORY OF
SWINDON'S STREET NAMES

Peter Sheldon
Richard Tomkins

RW—A

ISBN O 902633 62 7

Printed in Great Britain by Picton Print.

Citadel Works, Bath Road, Chippenham, Wiltshire

Contents

"The long and winding Road that leads to your
door will never disappear ..."

Lennon and McCartney

Drove Road (1926)

Guide to the Book

Street names give us valuable clues to the way of life of the generations
that have gone before us; their trades, their beliefs, their political
allegiances and their personal fancies. This book uses the medium of
street names to interpret the past events of a modern industrial town
and to place them in a historical perspective.

The streets of Old Swindon are examined first. Here we find such gems
as Windmill Street, Brock Hill and Horse Fair, names with their roots
deep in the Middle Ages. A cursory examination of these three names
tells something about the town's features, its wildlife and its customs
in the days before the Industrial Revolution.

The impact on the town of the advent of the Great Western Railway and
the opening of its locomotive workshops is assessed in the following
section, which deals with the myriads of streets that sprung up from
the 1840s onwards. We meet builders like Whitehead and Crombey, men
whose enterprise helped to turn Swindon into the 'Chicago of the Western
Counties' as Richard Jefferies called it! Modern streets are also covered
many of which prove to have origins of equal curiosity to the older ones.

Thirdly, Swindon's housing estates are surveyed. Resulting from the
town's post-war expansion, each estate has an individual theme for its
street names.

The book is illustrated with a series of line drawings that sensitively
capture facets of the town's history. These range from nostalgic out-
lines of thatched cottages in Old Town to the stark angular Murray John
Tower that dominates our present day skyline.

A substantial photograph section is included to compliment the text. The
photographs cover a wide range of Swindon streets - many published here
for the first time - shown as they were in the days of our grandfathers.
Included are scenes of boating on the now long forgotten Beatrice Street
Lake and the floods in Cromwell Street following a cloudburst in July

1922 when the water was nearly 2 feet deep and huge hailstones fell on the town. Also included are photographs of the famous men who for better or for worse have achieved a kind of immortality in bricks and mortar, ranging from Sir Francis Drake to Harold Fleming.

The book comprises a complete record of all the streets and roads within the boundaries of the former Borough of Swindon. As such it should appeal to all Swindonians new and old, to the casual reader as well as the historian.

The date that each street was named appears after each entry (except for the pre-industrial streets). The sources for this information are as follows:

1840-76   Kelley's Post Office Directory for Wiltshire
           Moore's Loyal Almanac for Swindon and District
           *Local Board Minutes
1877-1953 North Wilts Directory
           *Local Board Minutes (applies pre 1897 only)
1954 on   Electoral Registers

Where we have been unable to trace explanations for names, or where explanation is obvious, the street name and date only are given.

1.
Introduction

The often heard statement that 'History is all around you' rings especially true in the realm of street names. The old blue and white enamelled and latterly black and white metalled signs can reveal to the passer-by a wealth of interesting and sometimes unusual facts and stories concerning the history of their town or city.

Swindon is no exception. The street names here follow separate themes - hardly surprising, as the town comprised two separate communities, divided culturally as well as geographically, until the end of Victoria's reign. The pattern of names in the Old Town refecting the age of pre-industrial crafts and concerns. Here we find Market Square, Old Mill Lane and The Quarries, names that perpetuate the rural nature of what was for centuries a small hilltop village. Old Town remembers too, the very different social pattern of byegone days when the majority of people may or may not have 'blessed the Squire and his relations'. The Goddard family owned most of the town for centuries. What remains of their presence today can be seen in street names such as Goddard Avenue, Lethbridge Road and Pleydell Road.

A mile or so down the hill the town of New Swindon was rapidly expanding based around the GWR Railway Works. Not surprisingly, the Railway supplied, at first, the names for the streets. Those nearest the Works were named after stations on the GWR Line; Bath, Taunton, Oxford and Reading Streets. Then, as a tradition for quality and fine craftsmanship grew in the town, our grandfathers were proud to give the row upon row of new terraced houses names of GWR stalwarts, often men of genius, such as Brunel, Gooch, Armstrong Churchward and Collett. However, it was not only the great ones who were commemorated, the humble also achieved a kind of immortality. Cannon Street marks the spot were GWR signalman Tom Cannon built his house in 1879. The New Town prospered and so did the people. A lively group of middle class business-men soon appeared who were more than willing to invest in the building boom of the 1890s, a boom that saw the total number of streets in the Old and New Towns increase by over 70%. Their Victorian self-confidence ensured that we remember them today. Morse Street, Deacon Street and Whitehead Street commemorate such people.

In general, the town has its fair share of unusual names. The street known as Little London marks the area where a small migrant population from the capital made their home sometime early in the 19th Century, proving the idea of Swindon as an overspill town is older than was thought. The name 'The Planks' commemorates the old Wiltshire name for a flagstone. Such flagstones were once used to pave the raised footpath necessary in the lane leading to the old Holy Rood Church, a lane that quickly flooded in wet weather. The Church has long since gone but the lane is still known as 'The Planks'.

Swindon's streets show a lack of fanciful names and in the main there is a marked absence of names of specific events of our past. There are no Rosemary Lanes or Jackdaw Closes in Swindon; the nearest we come to romanticised names are the pre-railway titles Prospect and Brock Hill. These names have an almost prosaic quality that reflect a parochial pre-occupation that one would expect in a small closed community little concerned with the outside world. You won't find a Trafalgar Terrace or Waterloo Place in Swindon. However, the railway and the benefits of compulsory education changed things and brought the outside world a little nearer home. By the end of the century, Gladstone, Salisbury, Buller and Ladysmith had made their appearance in the Wiltshire country-side.

After the close of the First World War, the planned Council Estates began to appear. The Pinehurst estate was the first in the mid 1920s. Perhaps the names chosen reflect the cheery optimism of a socialist utopia in a land that was to be 'fit for heroes'. Limes Avenue, Beech Avenue and Acacia Grove, certainly hoped to take the town forward - even the names look to the future - no names here to remind us of past personalities or events.

An arbitrary naming policy seems to have been chosen for the more modern estates built since the end of the Second World War. Wiltshire villages (Penhill), GWR Locos (Park South) and Tudor statesmen/sailors (Walcot), have presented a rather untidy pattern.

8

Perhaps the pendulum is beginning to swing backwards. Modern names such as Canal Walk (1972), Charlotte Mews (1971) and North Star Avenue (1972) have shown a concern to return to the names of the town's heritage.

Where we live is one of the most important factors affecting our lives. Our address is our environment and our environment shapes our lives whether we like it or not. Knowing what that grafitti covered sign at the top of our street, road, avenue, means may not help to pay the rent, but it can help us to understand a little more about the development of our surroundings.

Peter Sheldon
Richard Tomkins

Little London (1910)

2.
Pre~Industrial Swindon

It is difficult to imagine that Swindon, now a sprawling town of some 100,000 inhabitants, was once no more than a sleepy little settlement on the top of a hill. A handful of narrow streets, an unusual medieval church and a rather ornate manor house - that was basically Swindon. Situated well off the beaten track, the events of the world seemed to give the town a wide berth, while strangers must have passed through with hardly a second glance.

This is not to say that the early history of Swindon is dull or un-important; when put into historical perspective, the more recent phenomena associated with the town's expansion appear all the more impressive.

The older streets and lanes of Swindon gradually acquired their names over the centuries, and it is virtually impossible to say when a name first came into use. Instead, we must rely on old documents and records to look for the earliest known mention of a particular street. This will give us a rough idea of the street's antiquity, although the name itself may have been in use for many years before that date. For ex-ample, the earliest reference to a Swindon street is to "Nyweport Street" in 1342, but this does not imply that it is the town's oldest street; High Street, undoubtedly an older thoroughfare, does not appear 'officially' until 1581.

The lack of official names and nameplates meant that streets were often known by more than one name, depending on the local features, landmarks or other means of identifying the locality. What the horse-rider would call Blacksmith's Street, the miller might know as Windmill Street, until such time as a single name was adopted for common use. Where names have been in use for hundreds of years, they are often corrupted by the vagaries of local dialect and phonetic spelling: 'damson' becomes 'dammas', 'Oak House' becomes 'Okus', etc.

"... but a small place, though the houses one (sic) well built, and of stone".

Universal British Directory of Trade, Commerce and Manufacture (1792-8).

BROOME MANOR LANE

A very old name that has probably existed as long as the manor itself. Named after the broom which grew here, the manor is first mentioned in the 1242 Book of Fees, when it was held by the Abbess of Martigny. Granted to Edward Seymour at the time of the Dissolution of the Monasteries in the 16th Century it was eventually bought by Ambrose Goddard in 1840. The road marks the site of a ten foot high standing stone called 'Longstone', and a line of smaller stones. These were removed in 1860 and sold to the waywardens of Cricklade for repairing their High Street! At the time of Jefferies, the field around the lane was still known as 'Longstone'. The first residential development began in 1928.

CRICKLADE STREET

The start of the old coach road to Cricklade. The gradient was once much more severe than it is nowadays as it originally ran level with the raised stone footpath outside the Christ Church Almshouses, before plunging down towards Drove Road. The street was remarkably difficult to negotiate in the days of horse-drawn carriages. This resulted on one occasion in a particularly nasty accident to the Oxford coach; the brake failed to hold and the vehicle turned a complete somersault, killing one passenger and seriously injuring others. The street was known by its present name in 1663, while a document of 1645 refers to a lease of a tenement in 'Cricklett Street'. In 1773 the road was lined with trees which remained a feature of this way out of Swindon until the present century.

DEVIZES ROAD

This name was formerly applied to the whole length of Croft Road as well. The name first appears in the 1858 Loyal Almanac, when the earliest houses were built here. The part nearest Victoria Road was also known as Short Hedge (or Edge) after the hawthorn hedges which bounded each side of the road. Also known as Horse Fair from the horse sales which were held in this road before the opening of the Vale of White Horse Repository (see Hooper Place). Both these names occur in the 1852 Loyal Almanac.

DAMMAS LANE

Led to the damson orchard of the Lawn. The first known reference is in 1684, though the name is undoubtedly much older. Spelling has varied over the years. "Dammas" is presumably the local word for "damson".

DAY HOUSE LANE

Means 'Dairy House'. Day House Farm was the home of Jessie Badon, the wife of Richard Jefferies.

EASTCOTT HILL/EASTCOTT ROAD

Led to the outlying hamlet of Eastcott, situated where the bus depot in Corporation Street now stands - known as Estcote in 1276 and Eastcote in 1366 (see Westcott Place). Terraces of small cottages sprang up on the Hill from the 1850s onwards and the former name of Eastcott Lane was changed officially to Eastcott Road in 1891. Pronounced "Esscut".

FLEET STREET

See section 4.

HIGH STREET

First known in 1581. The name is a standard one for any town's main thorough-fare, though it is possible that the name derives from the street's actual physical height: this is supported by the fact that Old Swindon was known as High Swindon during the 13th Century, because of its prominent position. With Newport Street and Wood Street, one of the town's most ancient streets.

KINGSHILL/KINGSHILL ROAD

After the King family, local landowners and farmers. Robert le Kyng's farm existed near here as early as 1332.

LITTLE LONDON

The home of a small migrant population from the capital some time at the start of the 19th Century, proving that the idea of Swindon as an over-spill town is perhaps a little older than we thought. Known as Little London Lane in 1807, and as London Street in the 1855 Loyal Almanac. The road was the most direct route for Devizes - Cricklade travellers, and it is likely to have seen use by stage coaches when Cricklade Street became impassable in bad weather (see also Walcot Road). The stretch north of Church Road was once known as Back Lane. Victory Row, built in 1879 demolished in 1960, was a small terrace at right-angles to the street where the Swindon Motor Company's car park is now. Little London possessed until the 1960s, Old Swindon's last remaining thatched cottage.

MARLBOROUGH LANE/MARLBOROUGH ROAD

What is now Marlborough Lane was formerly Marlborough Road - the original coach road and the most direct route from Swindon to Marlborough, via the Downs. The Lane now ends abruptly at Evelyn Street, its former course towards High Street having been blocked by the construction of the Swindon, Marlborough and Andover Railway's goods yard in the 1880s. The 'top' part of Marlborough Road was known as Lower Town during the last century, while the 1855 Loyal Almanac refers to it as Marlborough Street. The present-day Marlborough Road was named when the first houses were built in the late 1920s; before this time it had been known as Coate Road. See Pipers Way.

MARKET SQUARE

Grew up at the important junction of High Street and The Planks, the approximate centre of Old Swindon. A market is known to have been held in Swindon as early as the 13th Century (see Newport Street), though it was not until 1626 that Charles I granted Thomas Goddard a Charter to hold a weekly Monday market and two annual fairs. The Square would have been the nucleus of the market, although the livestock sales would overflow into the adjoining streets. A Market Cross existed in the 17th Century, and Morris recalls stocks and a pillory being sited here; a small circular market house stood in the centre of the Square until last Century.

MILL LANE

So called in 1703, after the water-mill which stood on the River Ray until the 1920s. The first houses were built about 1927.

NEWPORT STREET

The earliest known reference to a Swindon street is to Nyweport Street in a document for a grant of a tenement dated 2nd July 1346. The name is thought to mean 'new market' and reflects Swindon's earliest attempts to gain importance in the world of commerce. Also known as Bull Street during the last Century after the Bull Inn which stood opposite the present-day Old Town Tavern. Evidently a hostelry of ill-repute, Richard Jefferies called the Bull ' a disgrace to the town'. Altogether 19th Century Newport Street did not present an agreeable picture; in 1828 The Court Leet (forerunner of our modern council) reported the footpaths to be 'very much out of repair'. The Reverend George Pilgrim who lived here, reported to the Public Health Inspector in 1851 that 'the atmosphere of my house is notoriosly unpleasant to all who enter it either in close or rainy weather'. So much for the good old days!

OLD MILL LANE

After the water-mill which once stood at the bottom of the lane adjacent to Holy Rood Church pond, the site of which can still be detected. A mill worth 4s. Od. is mentioned in the Domesday Book and it is probable that this is a reference to this site. The mill fell into decay during the 19th Century and was eventually demolished about 1850.

THE PLANKS

This lane became flooded in wet weather and a raised stone causeway was built for the convenience of church-goers to Holy Rood. The name derives from the flagstones which were used to pave the raised footpath and the coping of the retaining wall (which still exists), "plank" or "plankstone" being the old Wiltshire words for a flagstone. An entry in the Old Town Local Board Minutes for 1868 refers to the "Old Church planks".

PROSPECT PLACE

Could well have been inspired by the 18th Century Modern Universal British Traveller, which records that the village of Swindon commands 'a delightful prospect over several parts of Berkshire'. The earliest reference to Prospect Place that we can find is in the 1830 Pigot's National Commercial Directory, shortly after the first houses were built. For Prospect Hill and Road, see section 4.

STRATTON ROAD

Between Swindon and Stratton. Stratton Marsh, the former name of the area towards Green Bridge, is reputed to be haunted by a white-habited nun.

WOOD STREET

First known in the time of Elizabeth I - a lease of a tenement dated 1599 is the earliest reference. May be a corruption of Wootton (Bassett), but more probably the site of a timber yard or wood store. Morris knew the street as Blacksmith's Street after the two forges which once stood here; Richard Jefferies records that it was called Windmill Street after the corn-mill which once stood on the site of the Kings Arms Hotel.

Newport Street (c1900)

3.
The GWR Village

Swindon was rudely awakened from its pastoral slumber by the arrival of the Great Western Railway in the early 1840s. The establishment of the company's workshops on the marshy lowlands to the north of Swindon hill soon transformed the small market town into a major industrial centre.

Why was Swindon chosen by the GWR? Certainly the place was well-sited between London and Bristol for purposes of changing engines, and as a junction for the line to Cheltenham; there was also an adequate water supply. But would not Wootton Bassett, Didcot or Wantage have fitted the bill just as well? At the time, the choice of Swindon must have been fairly arbitrary: looking back, it seems inevitable.

The first significant expansion of the town was the construction of the housing estate for GWR employees, west of the newly opened junction station, in the 1840s. New Swindon, as it came to be known, existed for many years as a self-contained community. Just one of the railway company's far-sighted social provisions in the town, this 'village' of 300 terraced cottages was a conception years ahead of its time, though sadly not a precedent that was followed in later housing developments.

Work on the estate began in 1842 and was more or less complete by 1853; credit for its design is given to Sir Matthew Digby Wyatt, the architect of Paddington Station. The stone cottages are laid out in neat rows either side of Emlyn Square, which itself leads to the Works entrance in London Street. Maintained by the GWR, and latterly by British Railways, the estate was taken over by Swindon Corporation in 1966. The houses have since been internally refurbished and admirably restored to their original external condition.

The streets are named after towns and cities served by the Great Western Railway.

"It is well known that when Isambard Kingdom Brunel designed the Great Western Railway he put Swindon there with the specific purpose of being stopped at. Swindon has no other function except for trains to stop at it."

C.O. Jones in "Vole" December 1978

BATHAMPTON STREET

Named Bath Street until 1901 when the suffix was added to avoid confusion with Bath Road in Old Town.

CHURCH PLACE

So-called because of its proximity to St. Mark's Parish Church, designed by George Gilbert Scott and opened in 1845. Also known as Park Road during its early years.

BRISTOL STREET

The former GWR school stands here. Built in 1845 at the same time as the rest of the street, it was closed in the 1870s upon the completion of the new school in College Street.

EMLYN SQUARE

Named in 1900 after Lord Emlyn, a former Chairman of the GWR; previously known as High Street, New Swindon. The area behind the Mechanics' Institute was called Market Place, after the octagonal covered market which existed there from 1854 to 1890 (see Market Street). This was the shopping place for New Swindon and must have been a great boon to the populace in the early days. The construction of the building, with its inner and outer circle of lock-up shops, was unique at the time. It also had its own 'pub' known as the 'Hole in the Wall', which did a lucrative business in beer and stout.

EXETER STREET

FARINGDON STREET

Now part of Faringdon Road.

LONDON STREET

OXFORD STREET

READING STREET

The 'Glue Pot' pub here was known as the "Old London Stout House" in the early 1900s. It was a 'men only' pub and if a lady wanted a drink she had to go to the 'jug and bottle' for it. These were the days before Women's Liberation and Mrs. Pankhurst.

The Railway Village

4.
'The Chicago of the Western Counties'

It was not long after the advent of the railway that local builders,
businessmen and landowners came to realise that they were sitting bang
on top of an unexploited goldmine. Much speculative building took place
to cater for the continuing influx of workers to the GWR, and the new
town soon lost the neat, orderly appearance of its beginnings. The green
fields around the nucleus of the railway village were gradually swamped
by the scores of red-brick terraces as the local landed gentry sold off
their lands bit by bit to hungry builders. By the time of the 1861 Census
the population was 6,856 - four times the 1831 figure.

That Old and New Swindon were separate entities was a fact recognised by
the setting up of individual Local Boards in 1864. Even though the two
settlements were slowly merging as new streets began to fill up the meadows
which had once divided them, the actual administrative link-up did not
materialise until the formation of the Borough of Swindon in 1900.

As finance was sometimes difficult, terraces rather than whole streets
were constructed, by scores of small speculators. A walk round Swindon
reveals the names of these terraces on stone tablets affixed to the houses.
Once a complete street was built, renaming and renumbering would take
place; renamings were also required in 1900, as several common names
occurred in both settlements.

Swindon's building mania was at its fiercest between 1890 and 1900. This
mania had been delayed however, for three important reasons:- (a) the
reluctance of the Goddard family to put their lands on the market; (b) a

large proportion of Rolleston property was tied up in a legal wrangle and did not become available until 1885; (c) a depression at the GWR Works during the 1880s led to a lull in the need for new houses.

Had it not been for these factors, Swindon's growth during the Victorian era would have been even more pronounced.

The earlier names of roads created by Swindon's expansion are based mainly upon the personal whims and fancies of the builders. It seemed to matter little what a street was called as long as it could be distinguished from other streets. The themes chosen normally stem from subjects close to the developers' hearts - not necessarily very imaginative ones - such as their home town, politicians with whom they sympathised and, of course, themselves. No less than 38 streets in the town are named after local builders! Only a few streets of this age take their names from local features like fields and farms.

There is no apparent difference in thoroughfares called 'roads' or 'streets' (historically, a street is built up, a road is not). Changes in fashion are evident in the names given to new residential developments - the first Crescent appears in 1908, the first Avenue in 1924, the first Close in the 1940s, the first Drive in 1951 and so on.

Regent Street (c1910)

*"... the main street, which was a poor thing, filled
with cheap shops and sixpenny bazaars."*

J.B. Priestley 'English Journey'
(Commenting on Swindon)

ABBEY VIEW ROAD (1939)

View from here of the ruins of Blunsdon Abbey, a large house destroyed
by fire in 1904. Built in 1860 by Thomas Barrett of Swindon, it was
said to occupy the site of an older ecclesiastical building dating from
the time of Henry VIII.

AKERS WAY (1949)

Councillor Francis Akers lived at Moredon and was Mayor of Swindon when
the road was opened.

ALBERT STREET (1848 Kellys)

Named after the Prince Consort, married to Queen Victoria in 1841.
Victoria Road runs parallel. The "Rhinoceros Inn" was situated at the
bottom of the street in the middle years of the last century. According
to Large, writing in "A Swindon Retrospect" in the 1930s, it was a
notorious place, 'the chief resort of bad characters of every description'.
There was a large room at the back of the premises, used for "dancing, cock-
fighting, glove-fighting and almost every conceivable vice". Quite a pub!

ALBION STREET (1877 Astills)

The first houses in this street were built by the Albion Building Society,
who had their offices at Albion Terrace in Bridge Street. The name means
'Britain'.

ALEXANDRA ROAD (1908)

The street was constructed about 1880 and known as Queen's Road (after
Queen Victoria) until 1908 - this earlier name gave rise to the name of
Queenstown. The present name commemorates Queen Alexandra (1844-1925),
the wife of Edward VII.

ALFRED STREET (1899)

Either after Alfred Leighfield, the son of a local builder, or Prince
Alfred (1844-1900), Duke of Edinburgh and fourth child of Queen Victoria.

AMBERLEY CLOSE (1958)

After the Gloucestershire village. Nearby are Fairford Close and Kelmscot
Road.

AMBROSE ROAD (1937)

A popular christian name of the Goddard family. Swindon has had four
Lords of the Manor named Ambrose, the last of whom died in 1898 (see
Lethbridge Road).

ANDOVER STREET (1879)

Named after the Swindon, Marlborough & Andover Railway, incorporated by
an Act of Parliament in 1873. Marlborough Street adjoins.

ARGYLE STREET (1890)

Probably a mis-spelling of Argyll, which version occurs in the 1894 Rate
Book. After the Marquis of Lorne, who married Princess Louise, a daughter
of Queen Victoria, and subsequently became the 9th Duke of Argyll.

ARMSTRONG STREET (1899)

In memory of Joseph Armstrong, the Locomotive, Carriage & Wagon Superintendent of the GWR in Swindon from 1864 to 1877. Successor to Gooch,
Armstrong lived in splendour at Newburn House, named after his boyhood
home in Northumberland. His elaborate memorial can be seen today in St.
Mark's churchyard.

ASHFORD ROAD (1886)

One of the streets built on the Down Field having names associated with
Kent, the others being Folkestone, Hythe, Kent and Maidstone Roads. They
were built on land owned by Sheppard, a local brewer who retired to live
in Kent about this time. Sheppard's brewery was in High Street and had
been taken over by the well-known firm of R.B. Bowley in the late 1860s.

ASHWELL CLOSE (1955)

ATHENA AVENUE (1970s)

Athena was the protectoress of Greece and goddess of war.

AVENING STREET (1886)

After the Gloucestershire village.

AVENUE ROAD (1890)

The first street in Swindon to be planted with an avenue of trees.

AYLESBURY STREET (c1880)

Built adjacent to the Aylesbury Dairy Company's farm and cheese factory
(established in 1876), situated just east of the junction station. This
also explains the origin of the Milk Bank, the name given to the railway
embankment here.

BANKSIDE (1971)

Built on the north-west slope of Swindon Hill.

BARBURY CLOSE (mid 1940s)

Known as Barbury Drive until 1963; after local Barbury Castle.
Baydon Close and Foxhill Close adjoin.

BARNFIELD ROAD (1958)

BARRYGLEN CLOSE (1973)

On the Elgin Estate.

BARTON ROAD (1948)

BATH ROAD (1850s)

Known as 'The Sands' throughout most of the 19th Century after the sandy
nature of the soil around the Portland stone quarries; this name was also
applied to what is now Okus Road. Eleven middle-class villas stood here
by 1841, built of Bath Stone cut from the excavations for the GWR. The
road was widened in the 1880s and the name changed officially to Bath
Road in 1904.

BATHURST ROAD (c1900)

One of five streets off Corporation Street commemorating Liberal politicians;
this one is named after Earl Bathurst (1762-1834), the M.P. for Cirencester.
See Gladstone, Graham, Rosebery and Salisbury Streets. Bathurst is also the
name of a Gambian river port - see Elmina Road.

BAYDON CLOSE (mid 1940s)

Known as Baydon End until 1963; after the Wiltshire village - see Barbury
Close.

BEATRICE STREET (1899/1900)

George Whitehead built many of the streets at Gorse Hill, and this one
is thought to be named after his wife. Whitehead was a man of many
occupations in Victorian Swindon; property speculator, builder, professor
of music and, from 1901 to 1916, landlord of the Princess Hotel in Beatrice
Street. In this latter capacity, George successfully converted the old
clay pit at the back of the pub into a pleasure ground and fishing lake -
called appropriately 'Whitehead's Lake' - to which he charged 1d. admission.
The lake enjoyed great popularity in the years leading up to World War I
and a photograph published in the Evening Advertiser in July 1977 shows
what a delightful place it must have been. Unhappily, the lake became con-
taminated and had to be filled in. Today the site is part of St. Mark's
recreation ground.

BEAUCHAMP CLOSE (mid 1940s)

Known as Beauchamp Grove until 1963. The Beauchamp family owned the Manor
at Lydiard Tregoze in the 14th Century. In 1430 Lady Margaret Beauchamp
married Sir Oliver St. John, bringing the estate into the St. John family,
an ownership that remained unchanged for over 500 years.

BECKHAMPTON STREET (1927)

Built in 1877, as a cul-de-sac off Princes Street and named Page Street after John Page, a haulier and builder who had his yard nearby. The old street was never one of Swindon's most salubrious spots and a new name was applied when the street was extended eastwards in the 1920s.

BEDWYN CLOSE (1967)

Named after the Wiltshire village to fit in with nearby Liddington Street.

BELGRAVE STREET (1901)

Possibly after the London street or Viscount Belgrave.

BELLE VUE ROAD (1856 Loyal Almanac)

The spot commands what once must have been a very attractive panorama over the lowlands to the east of the Old Town.

BELMONT CRESCENT (1908)

Literally, 'beautiful hill". Swindon's first Crescent.

BESSEMER CLOSE (1955)/BESSEMER ROAD EAST & WEST (1927)

After the engineer, Sir Henry Bessemer (1813-1898) the inventor of the Bessemer process for converting iron into steel.

BIRCH STREET (1892)

H.J. Birch was the accountant of the GWR works towards the end of the last century. In his capacity as Chairman of the New Swindon Local Board he laid the foundation stone of the Town Hall in 1890.

BOLINGBROKE ROAD (1949)

A family name of the St. Johns at Lydiard Park. Henry St. John, born at Lydiard in 1678 was created 1st Viscount Bolingbroke in 1712. He became M.P. for Wootton Bassett in 1701 and quickly rose in prominence to become Secretary of State by 1710. Bolingbroke was largely the architect of the Treaty of Utrecht that ended the War of the Spanish Succession in 1713. See also under Beauchamp Close.

BOSCOME ROAD (1949)

One of eight roads at Moredon named after southern holiday resorts. The others are Branksome Road, Cheddar Road, Lulworth Road, Poole Road, Shanklin Road, Swanage Walk and Ventnor Close.

BOURNE ROAD (1949)

After the local stream which gives its name to the parish of Rodbourne.

BOUVERIE AVENUE (1935)

Built on the orchard of the Lawn, home of the Goddards of Swindon. Named after Edward Pleydell Bouverie of Coleshill, Whig statesman and a director of the GWR.

BOWLING GREEN LANE (1962)

Leads to the green of the Westlecot Bowling Club.

BOWOOD ROAD (1933)

Bowood House, near Calne, is the ancestral home of the Lansdownes, Earls of Pembroke. Henry, 3rd Marquis of Lansdowne (1750-1863) and his grandson, the 5th Marquis, also Henry (1845-1927), were both eminent Liberal politicians of the 19th Century. The name was suggested by the wife of the builder of the road following a family visit to Bowood.

BRADFORD ROAD (1891)

Known before this date as Garrett's Lane or Back Lane. Laid out on the property of James Edward Goddard Bradford, a solicitor whose offices were in High Street. Still known locally as Bradford Lane.

BRAMBLE CLOSE (1950s)/BRAMBLE ROAD (1934)

A reference to the type of vegetation round here before the area was built up.

BRANKSOME ROAD (1948)

After the Dorset holiday resort. See Boscombe Road.

BRIDGE STREET (1855 Kellys)

Takes its name from the Golden Lion drawbridge which spanned the Wilts & Berks Canal, situated at the present-day junction of Bridge Street and The Parade. The bridge in turn was named after the legendary "Golden Lion" public house that stood close by on the canal bank. Much frequented by passing bargees, the pub's entrance was surmounted by a splendid stone lion which in later years stared benignly at passers-by from the canal towpath. This was a hazardous spot for a pub as men invariably fell into the canal at closing-time. They were fished out, no doubt speedily sobered up, by a man with a pole employed by the humanitarian landlords of the pub. A dangerous part of the town! Regent Street was also known as Bridge Street until about 1865. The two original terraces north of Fleet Street were known as Alma Terrace (after the Crimean War victory) and Bellewood Place; south of Fleet Street stood Albion Terrace and Crimea Cottages.

BRIGHT STREET (1884*)

Does not appear in the North Wilts Directory until 1891. Commemorates the radical politician John Bright (1811-1889) who, together with Richard Cobden, was instrumental in repealing the Corn Laws in 1846. Bright later became a Liberal M.P. and was partly responsible for the Reform Act of 1867 that gave many factory workers the right to vote.

BRIXHAM AVENUE (1958)

One of five roads off Upham Road named after south-west towns and villages, the others being Falmouth Grove, Merrivale Grove, Salcombe Grove and Thurlestone Road.

BROAD STREET (1901)

So-called because it is the main street of the late Victorian development between County Road and Corporation Street.

BROADWAY (1907)

The first houses appeared here about this time. Built on the site of
an old trackway forming a continuation of the Rodbourne Road from
Swindon. Known as 'bradan weg' as long ago as the year 943.

BROOKLANDS AVENUE (1936)

Refers to the nearby Rodbourne stream.

BRUCE STREET (1901)

After Sydney Bruce Morrison, a local landowner and solicitor, who financed
much of the building at Even Swindon.

BRUDDEL GROVE (1936)

A small close adjacent to Bruddel Wood; the land was formerly owned by
the Brudenell family, relations of the Ailesburys at Savernake   Lord
Cardigan of 'Charge of the Light Brigade' fame was a notable member of
the family. The locality is named Brudenell on an 1840 map, while
'Bruddle' occurs in the 1894 Old Swindon Rate Book.

BRUNEL STREET (1867*)

Named after the brilliant Isambard Kingdom Brunel, first engineer of the
GWR. Demolished about 1970, the site of the street is now covered by the
Brunel Plaza opened in 1972. See Gooch Street.

BRUNSWICK STREET (1906)

BULLER STREET (1901)

After Sir Redvers Buller (1838-1908), the British General who in 1900
relieved the town of Ladysmith during the Boer War, an event that
created almost hysterical acclaim in England.

BUTTERWORTH STREET (1892)

George Montagu Butterworth was a High Street solicitor who financed
several speculative building ventures during the 1880s. He was a
partner in the firm of Butterworth, Rose and Morrison.

BYRON STREET (1873*)

In memory of Lord George Byron (1788-1824), the famous poet and satirist.

CADLEY CLOSE (1974)

After the Wiltshire village; fits in with nearby Bedwyn Close and
Liddington Street.

CAMBRIA BRIDGE ROAD (c1870)/CAMBRIA PLACE (1886*)

The small stone cottages of Cambria Place were constructed in the early
1860s to accommodate the influx of Welsh ironworkers who were brought
to Swindon when the GWR's rolling mills were opened. The name is taken
from the mountains of their homeland. So scarce were houses at the time
that it proved impossible at first to house these workers. Fortunately
the GWR had erected a building known as the "Barracks" (subsequently a
Wesleyan Chapel and now the Railway Museum) as a communal dwelling-house
and there the Welsh immigrants temporarily took up residence. Large
records the curiosity this little Welsh settlement (many of whom spoke
no English) aroused especially amongst the younger generation. Nearly
all the Welsh families transferred to Cambria Place when it was completed
in 1864. The 1865 Rate Book records the settlement as "Welsh Colony".
For many years the services at the tiny Baptist Chapel here were conducted
entirely in Welsh. Incidentally, Cambria Place was the first area of
Swindon to have a piped water supply.

CANAL WALK (1972)

Part of the new Brunel shopping centre. Canal Walk incorporates what was
previously the western half of the Parade. A preserved canal-side mile-
stone serves as a reminder of the Wilts & Berks Canal which occupied this
site. Canal Walk was also the name given to the towpath here in the mid
19th Century (1861 Loyal Almanac refers).

CANNON STREET (1879)

The street was named after Tom Cannon, a GWR signalman, who built the
first house here. The street has links with Swindon's other railway,
the Midland & South Western Junction Line. It was originally planned
in 1873 that the line should leave the GWR station and be routed south-
wards by means of an 800 yard tunnel beneath Swindon hill, the entrance
to which was to be at the junction of Cannon Street and Victoria Road.
Construction actually started, but the scheme involved costly land purchase
and would have interfered with water supplies. The idea was scrapped and
in 1877 a route was agreed via Rushey Platt (the famous 'Loop'); the
line finally opened in 1881.

CARFAX STREET (1875*)

With Merton, Oriel and Turl Streets, this street was built by the Oxford
Building Society in a small field called Briery Close; named after the
Oxford street. The Oxford Building Society were responsible for several
other streets in Swindon - see Cobden Road, Dover Street, Harcourt Road
and Iffley Road.

CARLISLE AVENUE (1934)

Named after the Cumbrian town. Adjacent Corby Avenue and Scotby Avenue
take their names from two villages near to Carlisle.

CARLTON GATE (1975)

Built in Regency-style architecture in the fashion of the Carlton Club
in London.

CARLTON STREET (1877)

After Sam Carlton, manager of the GWR Works from about 1870 to 1895.

CARR STREET (1876*)

Now demolished. See following entry.

CATHERINE STREET (1875)

Possibly after St. Catherine. With Carr Street and Farnsby Street, built by the U K Land & Building Society.

CAULFIELD ROAD (1897)

CAVERSHAM CLOSE (1958)

Takes its name from the Berkshire village, as do nearby Swallowfield Avenue and Woodside Avenue.

CHANTRY ROAD (1970)

CHAPEL STREET (1886*)

Most of the houses were not built until 1902. Originally known as Chapel Lane and named after the Baptist Chapel of 1883 at the corner of Ferndale Road and Cricklade Road.

CHARLBURY CLOSE (mid 1940s)

Known as Charlbury Drive until 1963. After the Oxfordshire village. Nearby are Chilton Gardens, Coombe Road and Fernham Road.

CHARLES STREET (1884*)

The houses here were not built until about 1890. Charles Thomas was a local businessman who financed the construction of this and adjacent Thomas Street. Now demolished.

CHARLOTTE MEWS (1971)

Formerly an un-named turning out of High Street, leading to the Hermitage. Commemorates Charlotte Sanford, who married Ambrose Lethbridge Goddard in 1847.

CHEDDAR ROAD (1948)

See Boscombe Road.

CHEDWORTH GATE (1973)

Built in Cotswold style, this development is named after the Gloucester-shire village.

CHELTENHAM STREET (1870 Electoral Register)

Built by the Cheltenham & Gloucester Building Society; Gloucester Street runs parallel.

CHELWORTH CLOSE (mid 1940s)

After the Wiltshire village - see Barbury Close.

CHENEY MANOR ROAD (1929)

Takes its name from a one-time Lord of the Manor of Rodbourne, Ralph
le Chanu. The naming took place after Rodbourne Cheney became part
of the Borough of Swindon in 1928; prior to this date the road was made
up of four shorter streets: Telford Road, Swindon Road, Church Road
and The Green. Rodbourne Cheney has links with the Victorian novelist,
Thackery. His grandmother, Amelia Thackery, was the daughter of Captain
Richmond Webb, who owned the Manor in the 18th Century. Amelia was
godmother to the 'Emmy' upon whom the writer based the famous character
of 'Vanity Fair'. I wonder if Thackery ever visited the town of his
ancestors?

CHERHILL COURT (1963)

Laid out in the 1940s as Cherhill Lane and named after the Wiltshire
village. See Barbury Close.

CHESTER STREET (1888)

CHILTON GARDENS (1965)

After the Oxfordshire village; see Charlbury Close.

CHURCH ROAD (1888*)

Situated opposite Christ Church, built in 1851 and designed by Sir
Gilbert Scott.

CHURCH WALK NORTH & SOUTH (1937)

Church Walk first appears in the 1907 North Wilts Directory; it was renamed Church Walk South in 1937 when the northern section was constructed.
Leads to St Mary's, the parish church of Rodbourne Cheney.

CHURCHWARD AVENUE (1936)

After the great George Jackson Churchward (1857-1933), Chief Mechanical
Engineer of the GWR from 1902 to 1921. He has been described as the best
locomotive engineer England has ever had, and the achievements of his
'City' and 'County' class engines certainly support this accolade. First
Mayor of the Borough of Swindon in 1900/01, Churchward was ironically
killed by one of the engines he designed, whilst crossing the railway
from Newburn House to the works on a foggy morning. See also Collett
Avenue, Dean Street, Hawksworth and Gooch Street.

CLARENCE STREET (1893)

After Prince Albert Victor (1864-1892), Duke of Clarence and the eldest
son of King Edward VII. Princes Street is also named after him.

CLIFTON STREET (1879)

There is a steep cliff behind the Clifton Hotel which was formed by
excavations for railway embankments on the GWR, though the mural on
the Hotel's frontage would suggest that the street is named after the
Clifton Suspension Bridge in Bristol, designed by Brunel and opened in
1864. The street's builder was largely financed by Arkell the brewer.
The Hotel is reputed to be haunted, having been built on the site of an
ancient priory. The old name of the area was 'Cyprus' - perhaps a wood
of cypress trees once stood here?

CLIVE PARADE (1959)

After Robert Clive of India (1725-1774)

COBDEN ROAD (1905*)

The houses here were not built until about 1926. Laid out by the Oxford
Building & Investment Company and named in memory of their founder Richard
Cobden (1804-1865), a Liberal politician. Harcourt Road adjoins - see also
Carfax Street.

COLBOURNE STREET (1902)

A J Colborne, the builder, had his premises nearby in County Road. Note
the mis-spelling.

COLLETT AVENUE (1938)

Successor to Churchward, Charles Collett was Chief Mechanical Engineer
of the GWR from 1921 to 1941.

COLLEGE STREET (1877)

The GWR School was built here in 1873, near the modern Tesco supermarket.
The street probably took its name from the imposing Victorian school
buildings. Originally for girls only, College Street School passed into
the hands of the Swindon School Board in 1877 for a rental of 5s. 0d. per
annum. It provided generations of Swindon children with an education until
it was demolished in 1961 to make way for The Parade shopping precinct. It
is commemorated by a plaque and the original datestone which are set into
the wall of the passage leading to The Parade.

COMMERCIAL ROAD (1890)

Stood in the centre of the Rolleston estate, farmland that eventually
became available for development in 1885 (it had hitherto been the
subject of lengthy legal wrangling). Between then and 1901 this part
of the estate became a working-class suburb that took Commercial Road
as its axis. The road, with its new market house at the western end
(built in 1892) was so-named because it was intended to rival Regent
Street as the town's chief shopping centre.

COMMONWEAL ROAD (1928)

After nearby Commonweal School, the word meaning 'for the good of all'.
The 'Commonweal' was a Socialist magazine edited by William Morris in
the 1880s.

CONSTABLE ROAD (1959)

Named after John Constable (1776-1837), the Suffolk landscape painter.

COOMBE ROAD (mid 1940s)

Coombe Crescent until 1963. After the Oxfordshire village; see Charlbury Close.

COPSE AVENUE (1932)

Stands on the site of a small copse. With adjoining Wills Avenue, built by Colborne. He suggested that the two roads be called Chedworth Crescent and Wills Avenue however, the Council preferred Copse Avenue and Boundary Crescent - as can be seen, a compromise was eventually agreed upon.

CORBY AVENUE (1934)

Named after the Cumbrian village because of its proximity to Carlisle Avenue.

CORNWALL AVENUE (1937)

Near to Devon Road, Somerset Road, Surrey Road and Wiltshire Avenue.

CORPORATION STREET (1906)

Swindon Corporation's tramsheds (now the bus depot) were sited here and the original Corporation electricity generating station also stood nearby. Opened in 1903, the plant was replaced by the larger power station at Moredon in 1929.

COUNTY ROAD (1905)

Takes its name from the nearby County Ground, opened in May 1893 for football and county cricket matches on a piece of land secured for the town by Fitzroy Pleydell Goddard.

CRICKLADE ROAD (1890)

Known for some years previously as High Street, Gorse Hill.

CROFT ROAD (1904/5)

From Croft House, a large mansion built in 1841 where Hesketh Crescent now stands and later the home of Levi Morse. The house's two lodges still remain, one at the top of Croft Road, the other in Evelyn Street. Croft Road was formerly known as the Wroughton Road. See Springfield Road.

CROMBEY STREET (1891)

William Crombey was a local building speculator who developed much of the Rolleston Estate.

CROMWELL STREET (1866*)

After the Lord Protector of England, Oliver Cromwell. A complaint in
the New Swindon Local Board Minutes of 1866 refers to insufficient
lighting in the street. Now vanished beneath the Brunel shopping centre.

CROSS STREET (1877)

Probably after Richard Cross (1823-1914), a Conservative statesman and
Home Secretary, who devised the 1875 Cross Act for slum clearance.

CROSSWAYS AVENUE (1936)

Near to Stratton Crossroads.

CUMBERLAND ROAD (1928)

CURTIS STREET (1890)

William Curtis was a 19th Century builder, the partner of Davis.

DAVIS STREET (1893)

The 1891 Minute Book of the New Swindon Local Board records an application by A Davis to construct fifteen houses in this new street; Davis
went on to build many more of the houses in this area; see preceding
entry. Demolished about 1970 and replaced by an access road to the
Brunel Centre, later named Davis Place.

DEACON STREET (1891)

Hubert John Deacon was an Old Town silversmith and jeweller who bought
and built on this part of the Rolleston estate. His name can also be
seen on the north face of the Town Hall clock, which his firm constructed.
He died in 1929.

DEAN STREET (1890)

The predecessor of Churchward, William Dean was the GWR's Locomotive,
Carriage & Wagon Superintendent at Swindon from 1877 to 1902.

DEBURGH STREET (1902)

Laid out during the South African War, this street takes its name from
Colonel Ulick de Burgh (1855-1916).

DEVON ROAD (1937)

See Cornwall Avenue.

DIXON STREET (1876)

The Gorse Hill Brick & Tile Company built the first houses here and in
adjoining Stafford Street on a large field called Gilbert's Hill. The
area was not popular at first, because of the costliness of the property,
and the streets were only thinly built up by 1885.

DORSET GREEN (1968)

DOVER STREET (1876)

John Dover was a builder from Oxford responsible for much of the building around Prospect Hill. Presumably connected with the Oxford Building Society, he also built the streets in Briery Close near the Junction Station, see Carfax Street.

DOWLING STREET (1891)

DOWNS VIEW ROAD (1933)

View from here towards Liddington Castle and the Marlborough Downs.

DREW STREET (1907)

William Drew was the architect who designed the houses in this street; his offices were at 22 Victoria Street.

DROVE ROAD (1867*)

Probably called by this name before 1867. Formerly a lane up which the drovers would lead their sheep to market (see Walcot Road); also known as The Drove, a name which has persited to this day. The old name for the part of the road nearest Old Town was Brock Hill, 'brock' being the old English word for badger; these animals must have made their setts on the sandy hillside here. Variations of the name are Brokle Hill, Brockwell (1638 - after the nearby Holy Well) and Brockwell Hill (1865 Loyal Almanac refers). The old name continued in local use until well into this century.

DRYDEN STREET (1897)

After the poet, John Dryden (1631-1700). Milton Road, Shelley Street and Tennyson Street are other streets in the vicinity with the same theme.

DUDMORE ROAD (1928)

From Dudmore Lodge, a farm on the Wiltshire Downs near Aldbourne. Suggested by Mrs. Eugenia Goddard, the last inhabitant of The Lawn; Dudmore, Upham and Walcot were all farms on her late husband's estate.

DUMBARTON TERRACE (1897)

DUNBEATH ROAD (1974)

Dunbeath is a village in north-east Scotland. See Elgin Drive.

DURHAM STREET (1902)

One of the four streets off Groundwell Road named after Cathedrals, the others being Leicester Street, Lincoln Street and Wells Street.

EAST STREET (1869*)

Built at the east end of the GWR estate on part of Sheppard's Field. The locality is recorded as East Place in the 1863 Loyal Almanac.

EASTERN AVENUE (1935)

At the time of its construction this road formed the eastern edge of
Swindon's residential development.

EASTVILLE ROAD (1961)

Possibly after Eastville in Bristol.

EDGEWARE ROAD (1877)

Built by H.C. Smith of Edgeware Road in London. Islington Street adjoins.

EDINBURGH STREET (1892)

After the nearby Duke of Edinburgh pub, built in the 1870s and named after
Prince Alfred, Duke of Edinburgh and fourth child of Queen Victoria.

EDMUND STREET (1894)

Built by James Maxwell and named after another Swindon builder, Edmund
Jones. Jones himself built Maxwell Street, so some degree of mutual
admiration must be implied.

ELBOROUGH ROAD (1950)

The bridge over the River Ray on the Purton road is known as Elborough
Bridge, derived from 'elver', an old name for a swan. Known in the 17th
Century as Elvers Bridge.

ELGIN DRIVE (1970)

One of several roads on the Elgin estate named after Scottish places,
presumably because of the proximity of Edinburgh Street. See Barryglen
Close, Dunbeath Road, Lossie Road and Moray Road.

ELMINA ROAD (1899)

After the West African coastal town of Elmina. Gambia, Lagos and Volta
Streets have similar derivations.

EUCLID STREET (1899)

A name connected with learning was evidently thought apt for the new road
and school here; Euclid, the famous Greek mathematician, inspired the
names for both.

EVELYN STREET (1904)

Built on land belonging to Levi Morse, of The Croft, the street probably
takes its name from a member of his family. Led to The Butts, a field
used in olden times for archery practice and later the venue for Swindon
Town Football Club's home games before the County Ground was built.

EXMOUTH STREET (1883)

FAIRFORD CRESCENT (1936)

With Amberley Close, named after the Gloucestershire village.

FAIR VIEW (1881)

From Fair View House here. The spot commands a striking view over the centre and north of Swindon.

FALMOUTH GROVE (1958)

See Brixham Avenue.

FARINGDON ROAD (1890)

Incorporates Faringdon Street, Bath Terrace, St. Anne's Terrace and the northern terrace of Cambria Place; the renaming took place to avoid confusion between houses in the road with the same numbers.

FARNSBY STREET (Early 1870s)

FERNDALE ROAD (1889*)

Named by the Welsh migrants who came to work at the GWR after a small village in the Rhonnda Valley. A house in the road, dated 1889, is named 'The Ferns'.

FERNHAM ROAD (mid 1940s)

Known as Fernham Grove until 1963. After the Oxfordshire village; see Charlbury Close.

FIELD RISE (1960)

Situated on the southern slope of Swindon hill.

FITZROY ROAD (1937)

After Fitzroy Pleydell Goddard (d. 1927), the last of the Goddard family to live in Swindon.

FLEET STREET (1860s)

Despite the nearness to Regent Street, the name does not come from the London street. The track here was known as 'le flet' in 1600, after the old English word for stream. Fleete Way is mentioned in an Enclosure Act of 1657, while commercial directories record Fleetway in 1856 and Fleet Lane in 1865. The modern Co-operative premises, Fleetway House, perpetuate the older name.

FLEMING WAY (1958)

Commemorates Harold Fleming (d. 1955), the celebrated striker and Captain of Swindon Town Football Club in the early part of this Century.

FLORENCE STREET (1894)

Florence was George Whitehead's daughter.

FOLKESTONE ROAD (1892)

See Ashford Road.

FONTHILL WALK (1956)

After the Wiltshire village.

FORD STREET (1895)

William Ford had a builder's yard in Wellington Street and constructed the houses here.

FOSSE CLOSE (1961)

This and adjacent Watling Close are named after Roman roads.

FOXHILL CLOSE (mid 1940s)

Known as Foxhill Lane until 1963. After Foxhill near Wanborough; see Barbury Close.

GAMBIA STREET (1906)

The name derives from the West African country - see Elmina Road.

GANTON WAY (1972)

GEORGE STREET (1891*)

Does not appear in the North Wilts Directory until 1901. The firm of T. & J. George built many of the late 19th Century houses in Swindon, including the first terraces in this street.

GIPSY LANE (1884*)

A favourite haunt of gipsies in the days before the area was built up.

GLADSTONE STREET (1887)

After William Gladstone (1809-98), the Liberal politician and British statesman. See Bathurst Road. The name appears in the Town Clerk's Advertisement Book as early as 1874.

GLENWOOD CLOSE (1957)

Backs on to the Great Copse, a large wood which once formed part of the Goddard estate.

GLOBE STREET (c1906)

Globe Field once occupied the land between this street and Eastcott Road, where the Globe Inn stands. Frederick Large records that circuses were once held here; the field was in fact known as Circus Field in the early part of this century. Globe is probably a corruption of 'glebe', in other words, land belonging to the church.

GLOUCESTER STREET (1874*)

See Cheltenham Street.

GODDARD AVENUE (1899)

The Goddards were owners of the Manor of Swindon from 1560 until the 1920s and some land in the town is still in the possession of the Goddard Estate. The family has been in North Wiltshire since at least 1300 and can be traced back in Swindon with certainty to the early 15th Century. It is thought that the reference to one 'Wadard' in Swindon's Domesday Book entry may refer to an early member of the family. As Lords of the Manor, the family resided until 1931 at The Lawn, a fine Georgian house, sadly demolished in 1952. Many of Old Town's streets take their names from members of the family; Ambrose, Fitzroy, Lethbridge, Pleydell and Bouverie Roads and Charlotte Mews are examples. Goddard Avenue itself was laid out on land owned by Ambrose Lethbridge Goddard and is the highest point in the town. The thatched pavilion of Swindon Rangers Cricket Club formerly stood behind number 155.

GOOCH STREET (c1880)

Sir Daniel Gooch (1816-89) was the first Locomotive, Carriage and Wagon Superintendent of the GWR at Swindon, a post he held from 1837 to 1864; he and Brunel may be regarded as the virtual founders of modern-day Swindon. Gooch is also commemorated by the Sir Daniel Arms in Fleet Street. His successors were Armstrong, Dean, Churchward, Collett and Hawksworth.

GORDON GARDENS (c1890)/GORDON ROAD (1889*)

In memory of General Charles Gordon (1833-85), heroically killed whilst defending Khartoum against the forces of the Mahdi. Not surprisingly, Gordon became a popular hero in Victorian England - the Queen herself faithfully kept the General's Bible by her bedside. Gordon Gardens was known until 1894 as Fullesden Street.

GRAHAM STREET (1899/00)

Sir James Graham (1792-1861) was a British Liberal politician. See Bathurst Road.

GRANVILLE STREET (1892)

Built just after the death of Earl Granville (1815-91), a 19th century politician and Foreign Secretary under Gladstone. Levi Morse, a prominent Liberal, financed the construction of this and nearby Morley Street.

GREEN BRIDGE ROAD (late 1960s)

The site of Stratton Green, Green Bridge was the stone bridge over the Wilts & Berks Canal (built c1805), situated just south of the present railway bridge. The locality was also known as Stratton Marsh - Stratton Road refers.

GREENHILL ROAD (early 1940s)

A field here was called Greenehills as far back as 1630.

GREYWETHERS AVENUE (1938)

'Greywether' is the Wiltshire name for the sarsen stones which litter the fields in many parts of the county. Several fine specimens were unearthed here during building work and now form an attractive feature of the road's central green.

GROSVENOR ROAD (1913/14)

Probably named after Richard Grosvenor, Baron Stalbridge, who died in 1912. He was a railway administrator and an early advocate of the Channel Tunnel.

GROUNDWELL ROAD (1891*)

Possibly connected with the farm of the same name at Upper Stratton.

GROVELANDS AVENUE (1929)

Part of the cul-de-sac was built in the garden of 'Groveland', the large house on the corner of Springfield Road which was erected about the turn of the century by Edward Tudor Jones, a local solicitor.

GROVES STREET (1899/00)

John Groves was a brewer at Weymouth whose firm owned the adjacent Even Swindon Hotel. The firm was taken over by Devenish, who still own the hotel.

GUPPY STREET (1876*)

Does not appear in the North Wilts Directory until 1883. T.R. Guppy was one of the first directors of the GWR and Chairman of the company's pioneering committee; he owned land at nearby North Laines Farm (see Horace Street). A wealthy Bristol sugar merchant, Guppy was also a personal friend of Brunel. The 1885 O.S. map mistakenly shows Guppy Street as Jennings Street and vice versa.

HANDEL STREET (1899/00)

Apart from being a publican and builder, George Whitehead was also a prominent Swindon musician and dealer. He named the road after the celebrated German composer; his shop at 91 Victoria Road was called Handel House.

HARBOUR CLOSE (1958)

Probably named after an old field here. The name is commonly applied to any sheltered spot.

HARCOURT ROAD (1905)

Financed by the Oxford Building & Investment Company and named after Lord Harcourt, Liberal politician and MP for Oxford who died in 1904.

HARDING STREET (1873*)

Built on Sheppard's Field, just east of the railway village, one of
four streets here named after the landowner and brewer, John Henry
Harding Sheppard.

HARVEY GROVE (1936)

Albert Harvey was the farmer at Manor Farm until his retirement in 1935;
his son now lives in this road. Manor Farm was demolished in 1963.

HAVELOCK STREET (1866*)

After the British General, Sir Henry Havelock, who died after the
Indian Mutiny of 1857. Havelock Square, part of the Brunel Centre, was
opened in 1972.

HAWKINS STREET (1890)

Probably named after a local builder and musician called Hawkins.

HAWKSWORTH (c1976)

Fred Hawksworth was the last Chief Mechanical Engineer of the GWR, from
1941 to 1949. See Churchward Avenue.

HAYDON STREET (1876)

After James Haydon, Assistant Manager of the GWR Works at this time.

HAYDON VIEW ROAD (1961)

The road faces towards the outlying village of Haydon Wick, formerly
part of the parish of Rodbourne.

HEADLANDS GROVE (1935)

Takes its name from a local field, the 'headland' being the strip of
ploughed land where the plough turns at the edge of a field.

HENRY STREET (1873*)

According to the Victoria County History of Wiltshire Vol. IX, it was
formerly known as John Street. See Harding Street.

HESKETH CRESCENT (1957)

After Edward Hesketh Goddard, born in 1855, the son of Ambrose Lethbridge
Goddard. Built on the site of The Croft.

HILLARY CLOSE (1954)

Commemorates Sir Edmund Hillary, the first man to reach the summit of
Mount Everest. Tenzing Gardens adjoins.

HILLSIDE AVENUE (1931)

Built on the north-west slope of Swindon hill, just off Kingshill Road.

HINTON STREET (1890)

James Hinton (b. 1842) was a wealthy Swindon builder and Mayor of the Borough in 1903/4.

HOLBROOK STREET (1872)

Possibly refers to a stream (i.e. 'hollow brook') which once ran here, most likely the same one that gave its name to Fleet Street.

HOOPER PLACE (1973)

Previously an un-named turning leading to the rear of Skurrays Garage in Newport Street. Part of the land in this area was owned by Thomas Hooper Deacon, who held horse sales every other Monday at the Vale of the White Horse Repository. Deacon was Mayor of Swindon in 1908/9.

HORACE STREET (1892)

Built on land belonging to North Laines Farm; possibly after its owner.

HORSELL STREET (1891)

John Horsell built the first seven houses here on Frewin's Field. He was the landlord of the Rolleston Arms and Overseer of New Swindon Local Board during the latter years of the last century.

HUGHES STREET (1890)

Originally built about 1884 as Henry Street, the name later being changed to avoid confusion with the other street of the same name. After Henry Hughes, a speculative builder and beer retailer at Rodbourne.

HUNT STREET (1895)

Walter Hunt, a foreman in the GWR Works, built the first house here. Belle Vue Terrace, on the north side of the road, is the work of Thomas Turner and features the terrace's name in terracotta at each end.

HUNTERS GROVE (1904/5)

William Hunter, a Swindon furniture dealer, bought and developed this land. He evidently held his wife in great esteem as he named nearby St Mary's Grove after her. Hunter's premises were situated in Regent Street on the corner of Edgeware Road. An enterprising man was he - a 1905 advertisement stated that he would pay the railway fare of prospective customers wishing to visit his store! The shop is owned by a decorator's business today but the name 'W.W. Hunter' can still be seen in huge white letters in the brickwork on the side of the building.

HURST CRESCENT (1924)

The name means 'wooded hill'. Hurst Farm formerly stood in Whitworth Road. The locality was called 'Herste' in a document dated 1235.

HYTHE ROAD (1885)

After the town in Kent - see Ashford Road.

IFFLEY ROAD (1882)

Although laid out at this time, the houses were not completed until about 1890. Constructed by the Oxford Building Society and named after the Oxford suburb. See Cobden Road and Harcourt Road.

IPSWICH STREET (1906)

ISLINGTON STREET (1893)

So-called to fit in with nearby Edgeware Road. Cow Lane, a continuation of Eastcott Road, once ran parallel.

JEFFERIES AVENUE (1937)

In memory of Richard Jefferies (1848-87), the local naturalist and novelist. Built on the 50th anniversary of his death.

JENNINGS STREET (1883)

Possibly after General Sir Melvill Jennings (1841-1922). The street is mentioned in a Minute of 1875. See Guppy Street.

JOHN STREET (c1870)

Named after the landowner, John Sheppard, although separate from the other three streets which also commemorate him. Known as Chapel Street in its early years.

JOLLIFFE STREET (1891)

William Jolliffe held the post of Rate Collector for New Swindon Local Board at this time. Near to Birch Street.

JOSEPH STREET (1904/5)

Joseph Williams was a builder who had his yard at the corner of Newport Street and Devizes Road about the turn of the century; he built the first houses in Joseph Street.

JUBILEE ROAD (1950)

Commemorates the 50th anniversary of the Incorporation of the Borough of Swindon in 1900.

KELMSCOT ROAD (1937)

After the Oxfordshire village; see Amberley Close.

KEMBREY STREET (1907)

George Kembrey, a builder and haulier, had his premises nearby in Cricklade Road and owned part of the land on which this street was built.

KENT ROAD (1894)

See Ashford Road.

KILN LANE (c1974)

Leads to the site of an old brickworks off Cheney Manor Road. Previously un-named.

KING STREET (1865 Rate Book)

John King owned a building firm in Swindon during the 1860s so possibly named after him. Balances Queen Street, situated on the opposite side of Bridge Street.

KING JOHN STREET (1874*)

Presumably after the 13th century English sovereign. Laid out at the same time as Stanley Street and Victoria Road.

KING WILLIAM STREET (1871*)

William IV was King of England from 1830 to 1837.

KITCHENER STREET (1899)

Built just after the Battle of Omdurman, named after Herbert, Earl Kitchener, Field Marshal and Commander-in-Chief of the British Forces during the South African War. The house at the junction with Ferndale Road is called Kimberley House, after the site of Kitchener's famous triumph.

THE KNOLL (1923)

Built on raised ground to the west of Croft Road.

LAGOS STREET (1899/00)

Takes its name from the capital of Nigeria. See Elmina Road.

LAKESIDE (1957)

Overlooks the two artificial lakes of the Lawn, created by damming the Mill stream when the grounds were landscaped in the early 19th century.

LAMBOURNE AVENUE (1935)

After the Berkshire village.

LANSDOWN ROAD (1869 Electoral Register)

This road runs parallel to Bath Road and possibly takes its name from Lansdown Hill near Bath. The first two houses were built by Charles Morse; about this time there was an architect resident in Old Swindon by the name of Thomas Smith Lansdown, so if he designed the houses it is likely that the name commemorates him.

LEAMINGTON GROVE (1933)

LEICESTER STREET (1924)

See Durham Street.

LETHBRIDGE ROAD (1884)

Ambrose Lethbridge Goddard held the Manor of Swindon from 1854 to his death in 1898. Lethbridge was his mother's maiden name.

LEVERTON GATE (1972)

After the architect, Thomas Leverton (1743-1824).

LEWISHAM CLOSE (1963)

LIDDINGTON STREET (1928)

From the local village. Bedwyn Close and Cadley Close adjoin.

LINCOLN STREET (1910)

See Durham Street.

LINLEY CLOSE (1952)

Rumoured to be named after a member of the Goddard family to fit in with Ambrose Road, Fitzroy Road and Pleydell Road nearby. However, we can find no trace of any Goddard of this name.

LINSLADE STREET (1877)

A native of Linslade in Bedfordshire built the first houses in this street.

LITTLE AVENUE (1936)

William Graham Little, who died in 1924, was a well-known and respected local landowner and trader. He founded Little's clothes shop in Fleet Street in the 1870s, a business that survived the vagaries of trade until 1979. Little was also a philanthropist; he provided the land for the County Ground Extension recreation ground and gave scholarships for the poor boys of Swindon.

LORNE STREET (1891)

Possibly after the Marquis of Lorne, earl of Argyll (see Argyle Street).

LOSSIE ROAD (c1973)

Named after the river that flows through Elgin.

LULWORTH ROAD (1948)

See Boscombe Road.

LYNTON ROAD (1969)

A small access road on the Cheney Manor Industrial Estate. The land here is owned by Lynton Holdings Ltd., a London property development company.

LYNWOOD GROVE (1961)

Named after a large house which once stood on the side of the Purton Road, recorded as 'Lynnwood' on the 1922 6" O.S. Map. The name means lime-tree wood.

MAIDSTONE ROAD (1892)

After the town in Kent. See Ashford Road.

THE MALL (1906)

A stylish Edwardian name was chosen for this street, a mall being a tree-lined promenade.

MALVERN ROAD (1937)

MANCHESTER ROAD (1897 Town Clerk's Advertisement Book)

The first houses were built in this street during the 1870s, at which time it was known as Mill Street, probably after a nearby mill connected to Eastcott Farm. Originally a dead-end street west of Corporation Street, the new name was applied when it was linked up with Milford Street by demolishing part of the terrace on the east side of Wellington Street. The engineers responsible for this work were Maxwell and Tuke, whose main offices were in Manchester.

MANNINGTON PARK (1961)

Near to Mannington Recreation Ground. Mannington was formerly a tithing of Lydiard Tregoze.

MANOR CRESCENT (1949)

Built on the lands of Manor Farm at Rodbourne. See Harvey Grove.

MANOR ROAD (1892*)

Formerly known as Manor Terrace. Built on a turning out of Westcott Place which led to Westcott (Manor) Farm, situated where the Unigate Dairy now stands.

MANTON STREET (1917)

Actually built during the 1870s and named William Street. It remained a private street until it was taken over by the New Swindon Board in 1888 and renamed Marner Street, after H.G. Marner, the previous owner, who expressly asked for this to be done. The name was changed to Manton Street in 1917. The houses were demolished in 1969 and replaced by flats.

MARKET STREET (1891*)

The adjoining market was opened in 1892 by the Local Board to replace
the outdated and cramped GWR market on the railway estate (see Emlyn
Square). It was roofed over in 1903 and eventually demolished in 1977.

MARLBOROUGH ROAD (1928)

See section 2.

MARLBOROUGH STREET (1879)

Refers to the Swindon, Marlborough & Andover Railway. See Andover Street.

MARSLAND ROAD (1938)

MASEFIELD AVENUE (1952)

Commemorates the 15th Poet Laureate, John Masefield (1878-1967).

MAXWELL STREET (1890)

James Maxwell was a partner of Maxwell & Tuke, a firm of civil engineers
and surveyors to the Rolleston Estate. See Manchester Road. The first
houses here were constructed by Edmund Jones.

MEDGBURY PLACE (1912)/MEDGBURY ROAD (1878)

Built on two fields in the former parish of Eastcott known as Great and
Little Medgeberry. The first development took the form of a terrace and
stables for the use of bargees and their horses from the adjacent Wilts
& Berks Canal. Built in the 1840s, this terrace was called Cetus Buildings
and contained the 'Whale Inn' ("cetus" in Latin means "whale"). This
hostelry took its name from nearby Whale Bridge, so-called because of its
hump-backed shape. The name is perpetuated by the present-day Whale Bridge
roundabout here. The end terrace of Medgbury Road, facing the roundabout
shows a splendid mural by local artist Ken White, depicting the Golden
Lion Bridge (see Bridge Street) as it was c1908.

MERRIVALE GROVE (1958)

Merrivale is a village on Dartmoor. See Brixham Avenue.

MERTON STREET (1873*)

Named after the Oxford Street; Carfax Street refers.

MILFORD STREET (c1880)

Possibly an old name for the locality, associated with Mill Street (now
Manchester Road) nearby.

MILLBUCK CLOSE (1973)

MILTON ROAD (1895)

After the poet, John Milton (1608-74); Shelley Street and Tennyson Street are nearby. The story is that the association with the blind poet comes from a certain E. Jones, a blind tradesman who occupied the premises at the corner of Faringdon Road. A romantic idea, but in all probability merely fanciful. Laid out with Commercial Road, originally as a continuation of Victoria Road.

MONTAGU STREET (1906)

Montagu Butterworth was a partner of the Old Town firm of Butterworth, Rose & Morrison, who financed a number of private housing developments at the end of the last century.

MONTROSE CLOSE (1968)

MORAY ROAD (1973)

The Moray Firth is on the N.E. coast of Scotland. See Elgin Drive.

MOREDON ROAD (1906)/MOREDON PARK (1951)

Take their names from the suburb of Moredon, once a hamlet in the parish of Rodbourne. "Mordun" is mentioned in 943 and appears in the Domesday Book as "Mordone"; the name means 'marsh-hill'.

MORLEY STREET (1892)

Viscount John Morley (1838-1923) was a Liberal statesman and biographer of Gladstone. See Granville Street.

MORRIS STREET (1889)

The son of William Morris, W.E. Morris was a local builder who constructed several of the streets at Even Swindon in the early 1890s. However, perhaps it is the father whose memory should be perpetuated for the generations to come. Morris was Swindon's first historian and founder of the 'Evening Advertiser' in 1854. As a historian and writer his lively reminscences, published as 'Swindon Fifty Years Ago' in 1885, have provided countless Swindonians and newcomers to the town with a delightful glimpse of pre-railway Swindon.

MORRISON STREET (1899/00)

Sydney Bruce Morrison was a local landowner and solicitor who lived at No. 2 Clyde Villas in Bath Road. See Montagu Street.

MORSE STREET (1892)

The founder of Swindon's first department store, in Regent Street, Levi Lapper Morse was born at Stratton in 1853, the son of Charles Morse. He married Winifred in 1875 and bought Croft House in 1896. The second Mayor of the Borough of Swindon in 1901/2, he died in 1913 leaving two sons and four daughters. Morse also financed a number of building ventures in the town - the Local Board Minutes for 1890 record his application to build 28 houses in this street.

NELSON STREET (1897)

Either named after Lord Horatio Nelson, the famous British naval
commander, or Nelson Slade, the slightly less renowned Swindon builder.

NEWBURN CRESCENT (1936)

Built on the site of Newburn House, the residence of the GWR Locomotive
Superintendents (later Chief Mechanical Engineers). Newburn was the
Northumberland childhood home of one of the Armstrongs. Collett, on
taking up the post in 1921, those not to live here and the house was
eventually pulled down.

NEWCASTLE STREET (1908)

One of the six streets west of Drove Road named after English towns and
cities, the others being Northampton, Plymouth, Portsmouth and Southampton
Streets and York Road.

NEWHALL STREET (1891)

From the Birmingham business street of the same name. A contemporary
map inside the North Wilts Directory shows it as Spackman Street.

NEWLAND ROAD (1961)

Possibly a local field name.

NORMAN ROAD (1927)

John Norman was an Old Town builder who had his offices in Victoria Road.

NORTH STREET (1869*)

When built this street formed the northern limit of building in Old
Swindon, there being only fields between here and New Swindon.

NORTHAMPTON STREET (1924)

See Newcastle Street.

NORTHBROOK ROAD (1939)

As far as we can determine, there never existed a stream called North
Brook and this road is therefore so-named to distinguish it from nearby
Southbrook Street. Westbrook Street is similarly derived.

NORTHERN ROAD (1931)

Predictably leads to the northern outskirts of Swindon.

NORTH LEAZE CLOSE (1949)

Mention is made to North Leazes in a document of 1724, and an 1840 map
shows a field near Rodbourne called North Leaze. The farm of this name
stood by Rodbourne stream somewhere near the present-day Hreod Burna School.

NORTH STAR AVENUE (1972)

'North Star' was the GWR's famous broad gauge engine which hauled the
first passenger train from Paddington to Maidenhead in 1837. Withdrawn
in 1870, a part-replica was constructed in 1925 and can now be seen in
Swindon Railway Museum. The road occupies the site of the old Carriage
and Wagon repair shops.

OKUS ROAD (1888*)

First appears, in the North Wilts Directory in 1904/5. The name was
applied when the road began to be built up in the later part of last
century; prior to this time the track here was known as the Sands
(see Bath Road). 'Okus' is a much older word. Writing in a 1928
edition of the Evening Advertiser, Alfred Williams said that he believed
the word to be "... identical with an Aryan word meaning 'dwelling' or
'home' and therefore very ancient". The farm is recorded as Ocus on a
1773 map and as Oak House on the 1818 O.S. Map.

OLD MILL LANE

See section 2.

OMDURMAN STREET (1899 Town Clerk's Advertisement Book)

The Battle of Omdurman was fought in 1898 in the Sudan. Kitchener Street
adjoins.

ORIEL STREET (1876*)

After the Oxford Street; see Carfax Street.

OSBORNE STREET (1927)

Known as Osborne Terrace when the first dozen houses were erected about
1909. After the local architect and surveyor, William Osborne, who was
responsible for the construction of the Baptist Tabernacle and the
Victoria Hospital. His partner was William Read.

THE PARADE (1960)

A modern Shopping precinct on the site of the Wilts & Berks Canal.

PARK LANE (1888)

The name was applied to that part of Rodbourne Lane south of the London-
Bristol railway bridge, after the GWR Park here. A good class of cricket
was once played at The Park; Large recounts the times the immortal Dr.
W.G. Grace performed here, his team of eleven taking on and usually
beating a team of twenty-two locals. The standards of cricket in the town
declined after The Park was closed to the game when a large bandstand was
erected in the middle of the wicket! In more recent times, the Park was
the site of the annual children's fete, an event that undoubtedly gave
great pleasure to thousands of Swindon schoolchildren.

PARKLANDS ROAD (1939)

This land was formerly part of Park Farm. A field called The Parke existed in the vicinity.

PEEL WALK (1970)

A terrace abutting on to the old police station at Gorse Hill, known simply as Police Houses until 1970. After Sir Robert Peel, the founder of the police force.

PEMBROKE GARDENS (1927)

Both the Earl of Pembroke and Pembroke College at Oxford have owned lands at Rodbourne. The name appears on the 1922 6" O.S. Map, before the houses were built.

PEMBROKE STREET (1907)

PENHILL DRIVE (1951)

A farm called 'The Penne', later Penhill Farm, once stood here; it was the home of Adam de la Penne during the 13th century. Probably derived from the British word meaning 'head, top or height'.

PERCY STREET (1890)

PHILLIPS LANE (c1977)

Previously an un-named turning out of Devizes Road. Charles Phillips was a builder whose offices were at 16 Devizes Road; the Corn Exchange was built by him in 1866.

PINEHURST ROAD (1924)

Formerly Hurst Road, from the farm of the same name. The new name was adopted from a house in the road called 'Pinehurst' which dates from about 1910.

PIPERS WAY (1972)

From nearby Pipers Corner, the junction of Marlborough Road and Broome Manor Lane. The Pipers, a local family since at least the 13th century, owned the land here. The corner is said to be haunted by the ghost of a woman carrying a head in her hands.

PLEYDELL ROAD (1928)

Suggested by Mrs. Eugenia Goddard, the widow of Fitzroy Pleydell Goddard (1852-1927). Pleydell was the maiden name of the wife of Thomas Goddard, a 17th century Lord of the Manor.

PLYMOUTH STREET (1908)

See Newcastle Street.

PONTING STREET (1899/00)

Joe Ponting built many of the terraces which cover the Rolleston Estate.

POOLE ROAD (1951)

After the Dorset town. See Boscombe Road.

PORTLAND AVENUE (1947)

Situated next to the old Portland stone quarry in Okus Road which probably dates from Roman times. An outcrop of Portland stone forms the majority of Swindon hill.

PORTSMOUTH STREET (1909)

See Newcastle Street.

POULTON STREET (1892)

Presumably named after the Gloucestershire village.

PRINCES STREET (1876)

Commemorates Prince Albert Victor, the Duke of Clarence. Also known as Princess Street during the last century. Originally a narrow street linking Regent Circus with the Whale Bridge and lined with mean terraces, Princes Street has been transformed into a wide spacious dual carriageway.

PROSPECT HILL (1883)/PROSPECT ROAD (c1870)

Near to Prospect Place, so named because of the view from this point. Prospect Road was formerly Prospect Lane, known locally as Balch's Lane or Toomers Lane, after the dairy and coal yard of the same names. Before Victoria Road was built in the 1870s, the main thoroughfare between Old Town and New Swindon was through Prospect. Large remembers the days when the pedestrian from New Town had to climb the narrow path through Prospect to Old Town, crossing two stiles to complete the journey. These were the times before the lower town could boast adequate shopping facilities and practically the whole population was forced to wend its way up the hill on weekly shopping excursions. This was an event, according to Large, that caused the newcomers 'considerable difficulties'. He adds that they were 'rosy days for Old Swindon shopkeepers and publicans'.

PURTON ROAD (1928)

Officially named when the first houses were built, although this route to Purton was doubtless in existence for a long time before this date.

THE QUARRIES (1961)

Built adjacent to the Town Gardens; see following entry. First mentioned as "The Old Quarre" in 1641, the quality of the Purbeck stone dug here gave Swindon an important industry two hundred years before the arrival of the GWR. John Aubrey thought the stone 'excellent for paving halls, staircases, etc, it being pretty white and smooth'. Morris adds the information that the Quarries were extremely active at the beginning of

THE QUARRIES (continued)

the 19th century (canal construction etc) and that the 'whole of the
space on the western brow of the hill towards Westlecot was excavated'.
No. 14 The Quarries, is named Trout's Folly after a slaughter house and
row of cottages built near here by a certain Geoffrey Trout in the 1860s.
Apparently Trout constructed the slaughter house and found he couldn't
drain it properly - hence the name 'Folly".

QUARRY ROAD (1860s)

Situated in the midst of the old Purbeck stone quarries (now the Town
Gardens). The first houses were built for quarrymen on the twisting
access road between the two main quarries and known as Quarry Terrace
and Granville Terrace. The lane was officially given its present name
when the third terrace, nearest Westlecot Road, was constructed in 1906.

QUEEN STREET (1865 Rate Book)

Probably dates from about 1855; named after Queen Victoria. King Street
is opposite.

QUEEN'S DRIVE (1955)

Commemorates the accession to the throne of Queen Elizabeth II.

RADNOR STREET (1879)

Named after the 5th Earl of Radnor, William Pleydell-Bouverie, a
magistrate with local masonic connections. Known until 1883 as Redcross
Street.

RAGGETT STREET (c1876)

Henry Raggett was a grocer and tailor who had his shop at the corner of
Eastcott Hill and Stafford Street.

RAYBROOK CRESCENT (1967)

Adjacent to the River Ray, a stream which rises near Burderop Wood and
flows northwards to join the Thames at Cricklade. Ray is a variant of
'rea', a British word meaning 'something that twists and turns'. Known
as The Rey in 1576 and as Rye in 1754. Its previous name was the Worfe
(after which Wroughton is named), and it has also been known as the Key.

RAYFIELD GROVE (1904/5)

Near to the Rodbourne stream, a tributary of the Ray. See preceding entry.

READ STREET (1879)

After William Read, a local surveyor and estate agent, ..nose offices were
at the Corn Exchange.

REDCLIFFE STREET (1891)

Supposedly after the Redcliffe area in Bristol.

REGENT CIRCUS (1890)/REGENT PLACE (c1900)/REGENT STREET (1865)

The first houses were built on the southern part of Bridge Street (later Regent Street) and in York Place (the former name of the terrace in Regent Circus between Theatre Square and the Rifleman's Arms) during the 1850s. The present name, deriving from the London street, was bestowed about the time that the workers' cottages in the street were being converted to shops. Regent Circus was originally going to be called 'Trafalgar Square' but this was evidently thought a little too pretentious for a town such as Swindon. Regent Place stood near the site of modern Theatre Square.

RICHMOND ROAD (1933)

After the town in Surrey.

RIDGEWAY CLOSE (mid 1940s)

Known as Ridgeway Drive until 1968. After the ridge of Corallian Limestone which runs from east to west through the northern outskirts of Swindon. Ridgeway Farm once stood near here; 'Ridgwaye grounde' is mentioned in a document of 1635, while 'Ridge Way Mill' appears on the 1773 O.S. Map.

RIPLEY ROAD (1893)

Adjoins Bradford Road. James Bradford Goddard, the local solicitor, married Charlotte Beatrice Tyndale Ripley in 1885.

RIVERDALE CLOSE (1959)/RIVERDALE WALK (1972)

Close to the River Ray; see Raybrook Crescent.

ROLLESTON STREET (1873*)

Built on part of the estate of the Rolleston family, owned at that time by Colonel William Villett Rolleston who let the land out on leases to various speculative builders.

ROMAN CRESCENT (1958)

A Roman Villa was discovered in the vicinity when the houses in Westlecot Road were being erected in the 1890s. Excavated by A.D. Passmore from 1897 onwards, the villa is thought to have had some connection with the nearby Okus Quarries and had apparently been destroyed by fire.

ROMSEY STREET (1891*)

Does not appear in the North Wilts Directory until 1913.

ROSE STREET (1902)

Herbert Rose was a Swindon solicitor - Montagu Street refers.

ROSEBERY STREET (1899/02)

Takes its name from the Liberal politician, the 5th Earl of Rosebery
(1847-1929). The year 1894 was a good one for Rosebery; he served
as Prime Minister and his horse won the Derby - a unique double. See
Bathurst Road.

ST. HELEN'S VIEW (1973)

Overlooks the parish church of Wroughton, which is dedicated to St.
Helen and St. John.

ST. MARGARET'S ROAD (1897)

Laid out on part of the land adjoining The Croft and owned by Levi
Morse. He named the street after his birthplace, Stratton St. Margaret.

ST MARY'S GROVE (1899/00)

See Hunter's Grove.

ST. PAUL'S STREET (1890)

After the church here, built in 1881 and designed by Sir Arthur Blomfield.

SALCOMBE GROVE (1958)

See Brixham Close.

SALISBURY STREET (1899/00)

Robert Cecil (1830-1903) the Conservative politician was 3rd Marquess of
Salisbury and three times Prime Minister. See Bathurst Road.

SANDOWN AVENUE (1938)

SANFORD STREET (c1873)

Sanford was the maiden name of Ambrose Goddard's wife, Charlotte (1824-1904).

SARSEN CLOSE (1971)

Named in error after the large boulders which were uncovered during building
work and which now form an attractive feature of the road. The stones are
in fact calcareous sandstone doggers from the sandy stratum of Swindon hill.

SAVERNAKE STREET (1907)

SCARBOROUGH ROAD (1910)

SCOTBY AVENUE (1936)

See Carlisle Avenue.

SHANKLIN ROAD (1951)

After the Isle of Wight resort - see Boscombe Road.

SHELLEY STREET (1906)

One of several streets in the town centre commemorating poets; after
Percy Bysshe Shelley (1792-1822). Dryden Street is nearby.

SHEPPARD STREET (1873*)

Built on Sheppard's Field and named after the brewer John Sheppard, at
his insistence. Sheppard died in 1876 leaving £200 in his Will to be
invested for the benefit of twelve aged persons every Christmas. In
1904 the income, known as 'Sheppard's Dole' was £5 2s. 6d. See also
under Ashford Road and Harding Street.

SHRIVENHAM ROAD (1923)

Leads towards Shrivenham and once known as Stratton Road.

SOMERSET ROAD (1936)

Possibly takes its name from Edward Seymour, Duke of Somerset, who owned
the Manor of Even Swindon in the 16th Century. More likely is that the
name follows a pattern of county names popular in this area. See also
Cornwall Avenue.

SOUTH STREET (c1870)

Named because of its location in relation to North Street. During the
last century the eastern end was called 'Providence Road' after the
Providence Chapel here.

SOUTHAMPTON STREET (1924)

See Newcastle Street.

SOUTHBROOK STREET (1906)

Built on the site of a track which led from New Swindon to Southbrook Farm.
The name comes from a small tributary of the River Ray which once flowed
here. 'Sowbrooke Farm' is shown on an 18th century map. Southbrook Lane
appears in the 1891 North Wilts Directory.

SOUTH VIEW AVENUE (1939)

SPRING GARDENS (1888)

A well is shown here on the 1885 O.S. 6" Map, and a lake formed by a
disused claypit once stood in the recreation ground; however we can find
no evidence of a spring ever existing. Demolished in 1972 and renamed
the following year when the road was rebuilt.

SPRINGFIELD ROAD (1886)

Before the houses were built, the track here which led towards Westlecot
was known as Quarry Lane; the Old Swindon Minutes of 1884 record a planning
application to build six houses in Quarry Lane. The field which was situated
between Grovelands Avenue and Croft Road once held a spring, one of many on
this side of Swindon hill. The stream flowed into a stone trough hard by

SPRINGFIELD ROAD (continued)

Croft Road and provided one of the town's major water supplies until last century. The site of the trough is now marked by a stone plaque.

STAFFORD STREET (1876)

STANIER STREET (1891)

William Stanier was Stores Superintendent of the GWR at Swindon. Born at Wolverhampton in 1849, he moved to Swindon and lived from 1886 in The Sands (now Bath Road) becoming Mayor of the Borough in 1907/8. His son was the famous Sir William Stanier, Chief Mechanical Engineer of the London, Midland & Scottish Railway.

STANLEY STREET (1877)

After Sir Henry Stanley (1841-1904) the explorer of Africa.

STANMORE STREET (1893)

STATION ROAD (early 1840s)

Swindon Junction Station was opened in July 1842.

THE STREET (1928)

At one time this was Moredon's main road and was undoubtedly known by this name before 1928, the date when it first appears in the North Wilts Directory.

SUFFOLK STREET (1899/00)

SUMMERS STREET (1891)

About this time there was a beer retailer in Westcott Place named Summers and he possibly built the houses here.

SUNNINGDALE ROAD (1961)

This and adjoining Eastville Road are named after places in Bristol.

SUNNYSIDE AVENUE (1931)

Built at the foot of the hill near Okus and presumably named to sound attractive to potential house-buyers.

SURREY ROAD (1933)

SWALLOWFIELD AVENUE (1960)

After the Berkshire village of the same name. See Caversham Close.

SWANAGE WALK (1977)

See Boscombe Road

SWINDON ROAD (1880)

TEMPLE STREET (1888)

Leads to the Baptist Tabernacle, built in 1886, demolished in 1979.

TENNYSON STREET (1895)

After the poet, Alfred Lord Tennyson (1809-92). Leads out of Milton Road.

TENZING GARDENS (1954)

Named after the mountaineer, Sherpa Tenzing, who in 1953 climbed Mount Everest with Edmund Hillary.

THEATRE SQUARE (1971)

A modern pedestrian precinct adjacent to the Wyvern Theatre built roughly on the site of Regent Place.

THEOBALD STREET (1888)

THOMAS STREET (1884*)

Charles Thomas was a local businessman and building speculator.

THURLESTONE ROAD (1958)

Thurlestone is a village in south Devon; see Brixham Avenue.

TISMEADS CRESCENT (1934)

A field here was called 'Tidsmead' in 1641. The 1888 North Wilts Directory shows a Mr. Edward Gough as resident at a house called 'Tismeads'.

TITHE BARN CRESCENT (1958)

Named after the ancient thatched Okus Barn which stood nearby until its untimely demolition in 1975.

TIVERTON ROAD (1937)

TURL STREET (1874*)

Inspired by the Oxford Street of the same name - Carfax Street refers.

TURNER STREET (1893)

Thomas Turner was a local 19th century builder and brickmaker, also a director of the Wilts & Berks Canal Company. Turner's clay pits were situated in what is now Queen's Park, while he himself lived in the large brick mansion in Drove Road which is the present-day Grove Inn. Turner was responsible for producing the distinctive orangey-red bricks and ornate terracotta embellishments which make his buildings so immediately recognisable. The street name is in fancy brickwork at the terrace ends.

TYDEMAN STREET (1928)

W.H. Tydeman founded a building business in Edgeware Road in 1897.

UNION ROW (1865)/UNION STREET (1865)

The origin of these two names remains a mystery. A clue may lie in
the date, which marked the end of the American Civil War and the victory
of the Unionists over the Confederates. Perhaps the names perpetuate
that victory? Less romantically the name could also celebrate the
establishment of Local Boards of Health in both Old and New Swindon
in 1864; these Boards superceded the former Poor Law Unions.

UPHAM ROAD (1928)

After Upper Upham Farm on the Marlborough Downs near Aldbourne. Originally
owned by John of Gaunt, who used it as a hunting lodge, the farm passed into the hands of the Goddard family during the 16th century. See Dudmore
Road.

VALLEYSIDE (1974)

Named to fit in with adjacent Sunnyside Avenue and Bankside.

VANBRUGH GATE (1978)

Sir John Vanbrugh (1664-1726) was an English architect and the designer
of Blenheim Palace. The houses here, with their shutters and pan-tiled
roofs, imitate the English Baroque style for which Vanbrugh was best known.

VENTNOR CLOSE (1951)

After the Isle of Wight holiday resort; see Boscombe Road.

VICARAGE ROAD (1932)

By-passes the old nucleus of the hamlet of Rodbourne Cheney on land which
formerly belonged to St. Mary's Church.

VICTORIA ROAD (1848 Kellys)

The original street extended only from Bath Road to the junction with
Prospect Place and was known as Victoria Street. The idea of extending
it northwards to provide a suitable link between the Old and New Towns
was first put forward by the Old Swindon Local Board in 1871 and this
new road was constructed by 1875. The new section was initially known
simply as New Road, later Victoria Street North. In 1903 both the old
and new sections were renamed Victoria Road. The name, which of course
commemorates Queen Victoria, runs parallel to Albert Street.

VILLETT STREET (1876*)

The Villett family were Lay Rectors at Holy Rood in Old Swindon during
the 17th century and Lords of the Manor of Eastcott. The large amount
of property which the family owned later passed into the hands of the
Rollestons, who sold off their interests for speculative building purposes.

VOLTA ROAD (1897)

After the Ghana river port; see Elmina Road.

WALCOT ROAD (1928)

Built on the site of a bridle-road that led to the farmstead of Walcot. 'Walecote' is mentioned in the Domesday Book, the name meaning 'village of the Welsh'. William Morris records that the track was once part of a green road from Reading to Somerset along which drovers would herd their sheep from market to market - the route they took through Swindon was via Walcot, Drove Road, Little London and Okus. Before 1928 the track was known locally as The White Way. See also Dudmore Road.

WARWICK ROAD (1901)

Formerly the site of Hay Lane Cottages, a row of workmen's cottages originally constructed at Hay Lane, between Swindon and Wootton Bassett to house navvies engaged in the construction of the GWR. The buildings were later dismantled and re-erected on a site east of Eastcott Hill; they are first mentioned in the 1869 Rate Book. The lane which led to them came to be known as Hay Lane, and this still exists north of Warwick Road as a small muddy passageway between Eastcott Hill and Swindon Road.

WATLING CLOSE (1961)

After the Roman Road. Fosse Close adjoins.

THE WEAVERS (1978)

Recent archeological excavations nearby have revealed the remains of Saxon weaving huts, indicating that the weaving industry existed in Swindon on a small scale during the Dark Ages.

WELLINGTON STREET (c1870)

After the Duke of Wellington (1769-1852), victor of Waterloo and Tory Prime Minister from 1828-1830. Wellington Street marks the site of the historic Railway Mission. Built in 1903 as part of the Evangelical Council of Churches, it served to carry the faith to several generations of railwaymen. Sadly, this small part of Swindon's history was recently gutted by fire and has been demolished.

WELLS STREET (1899/00)

One of four streets here named after cathedrals. See Durham Street.

WEMBLEY STREET (1926)

Commemorates the opening of Wembley Stadium in 1923 and the subsequent British Empire Exhibitions held there over the following two years.

WESLEY STREET (1900)

Leads to the rear of the Bath Road Wesleyan Chapel. The road was built about 1877 at which time it was known as Chapel Street; the name was changed when Old and New Swindon merged to form a single Borough, to avoid confusion with the Gorse Hill street of the same name.

WESTBROOK STREET (1936)

To distinguish from nearby Southbrook Street.

WESTCOTT PLACE (mid 1840s)/WESTCOTT STREET (1878)

Westcott was once a hamlet in the West Field of Swindon; along with Eastcott, it formed part of the Manor of Nethercott. The houses in Westcott Place were the first private dwellings for railway workers to be built in New Swindon; their cramped, functional design is very similar to the contemporary development in Medgbury Road. No. 51 Westcott Place, in the width of its frontage at least, is the smallest house in Swindon.

WESTERN STREET (c1870)

Probably named after the Great Western Railway, affectionately known as 'the Western' to those who worked 'inside' the Works.

WESTLECOT ROAD (1886)

After the Manor of Westlecot, once a hamlet in the parish of Wroughton. First recorded in the Domesday Book, as "Wichelstok'. The Manor was held by the nuns of Lacock Abbey until coming into the possession of the Goddard family of Upham in 1541, shortly after the Dissolution of the Monasteries. The present Manor building dates from the late 16th century.

WESTMORLAND ROAD (1926)

WEYMOUTH STREET (c1870)

A former cul-de-sac off Wellington Street where the bus station now stands.

WHARF ROAD (c1892)

Ran alongside the Wilts & Berks Canal to a small wharf established by the New Swindon Local Board in 1892 at the end of Cromwell Street; the Wharf House survived into the 1970s. Now only a small length of road remains and this has been incorporated into Market Street.

WHEELER AVENUE (1935)

Reputedly named after a Gorse Hill landowner.

WHITBY GROVE (1934)

Built parallel to Scarborough Road; both towns are Yorkshire seaside resorts.

WHITEHEAD STREET (1892)

Named after George Whitehead, Victorian Swindon's man of many talents and one of the town's most prolific builders during the latter part of the 19th century. See Beatrice Street. At the turn of the century a shop called the Town Hall Stores stood on the corner of Whitehead and Curtis Streets. The shop sold jars of jam and marmalade covered with red labels showing a view of Swindon Town Hall. Truly a local industry!

WHITEHOUSE ROAD (1906)

Takes its name from the White House pub at the corner of Station Road
and Corporation Street; the pub was known as the Queen's Arms until
some time in the 1890s. The White House is currently painted blue!

WHITEMAN STREET (1890)

Built at Gorse Hill near the site of Jesse Whiteman's farm.

WHITNEY STREET (1892)

WHITWORTH ROAD (1904/5)

Sir Joseph Whitworth was a well-known machine-tool inventor whose firm
supplied the GWR Works with most of its equipment during the last century.

WICKDOWN AVENUE (1963)

Near to Haydon Wick, and probably named after a local field.

WILLIAM STREET (1878)

Named after the builder, William Crombey, who lived at No. 1.

WILLS AVENUE (1931)

Adjacent to W.D. & H.O. Wills' sports ground in Shrivenham Road. See
Copse Avenue.

WILTSHIRE AVENUE (1931)

WINIFRED STREET (1899/00)

Built on land adjoining Croft House, the home of Levi Morse; he married
Winifred Humphries of Broad Hinton in 1875 and named the street after her.

WOODLAND VIEW (1971)

The name given to the spur of Croft Road near the Black Horse Inn which
was formed when the new road bridge was built over the M4. Looks eastwards
to Burderop Woods.

WOODSIDE AVENUE (1955)

Situated at the foot of the hill where The Lawn woods stand. Woodside is
also a village in Berkshire (see Caversham Close).

WYVERN CLOSE (1967)

After the mythical medieval beast, the emblem of the Celtic and Saxon
kings of Wessex.

YARDLEY CLOSE (1966)

YORK ROAD (1907)

The first of the streets to be built west of Drove Road that are named
after English towns and cities. See Newcastle Street.

Photographs

1. GODDARD FAMILY

   A photograph of Ambrose Lethbridge Goddard and his family, taken
   around 1880. Lords of the Manor of Old Town, the Goddards gave
   their family names to many streets in Swindon. No less than six
   streets were named after those pictured here. Identifications
   are from left to right:-

Ambrose Ayshford	1848-1885	(seated)
Jessie Henrietta	1850-1920	(standing)
Ambrose Lethbridge	1819-1898	(seated)
Charles Frederick	1863-1942	(standing)
Charlotte (wife of	1824-1904	(seated)
Ambrose Lethbridge)		
Fitzroy Pleydell	1852-1927	(half-seated)
Edward Hesketh	1855-1921	(seated)

2. THE PLANKS

   The Planks led from the Market Square in Old Town to Holy Rood Church.
   As such it must have been one of the most important roadways in pre-
   railway Swindon. The GWR swept away the old patterns of life and an
   expanding population rendered Holy Rood obsolete in 1850, to be
   superceded as parish church by Christ Church. This has left The
   Planks a semi rural backwater tucked away behind the hustle and
   bustle of Old Town.

3. THE WHITEHOUSE

   At sometime in the 1890s the 'Queens Arms Hotel' situated on the
   corner of Station Road, was renamed 'The Whitehouse'. A decade later
   it gave its name to the newly built road that ran past its door -
   hence Whitehouse Road.

4. GREYWETHERS AVENUE

   Greywethers Avenue is an example of how local geographical features
   can influence naming. These fine sarsen stones, known locally as
   'greywethers' were unearthed when the houses were built.

5. CURTIS STREET

   Curtis Street has remained largely unaltered by the passage of nearly
   70 years. The splendid bay window of what was Franklins the decorators'
   original premises continues to defy the wheels of progress, as does the
   Rolleston Arms clock, still there today forever advertising the long
   departed firm of Cottell Brothers.

6. BROAD STREET - 1913

Broad Street is another area of Swindon that has escaped re-development. A visitor from Edwardian days would find this scene little changed today. Perhaps the young boy with the football is telling his friend about the goal Harold Fleming scored for Swindon the previous Saturday? These were the days when Swindon Town reached the semi-final of the F.A. Cup and humbled many great teams on the nearby County Ground.

7. COMMERCIAL ROAD - 1913

Originally intended as a shopping area to rival Regent Street, Commercial Road failed in this purpose as the photograph shows. By the First World War it was mainly a residential area with sporadic shops along its length. The tidy houses provided a neat uniform street, perhaps preferable to the hotch-potch of development seen here today. Ironically the street has now reverted to its original function as the commercial centre of the town.

8. LEAVING GWR WORKS - 1913

A study of GWR workers leaving the Bristol Street Works entrance was a common theme for Edwardian photographers. This superb study is the finest we have seen. I wonder if many of the children playing in the roadway are alive today? They have lived through two World Wars, and have witnessed such changes that our ancestors would not have thought possible.

9. CROMWELL STREET - 1913

The Fox Tavern, Briggs shoe shop and Cromwell Street itself have all disappeared, replaced by the new Brunel Centre. Marks and Spencer's and Lloyds' Bank in Regent Street, mark the spot where these shoppers stood and posed for the photographer. Different people in a different world.

10. FLOODS IN CROMWELL STREET

It seems that wet summers have always been with us. Here we see Cromwell Street on the day of the great flood: Sunday July 22nd 1922. An eye-witness reported: "It was about 1.45 pm .. The sky came over very black and it was so dark you had to have all the house lights on.. The next thing we knew huge hailstones were falling and then the rain came pelting down". In fact, it rained so heavily for more than an hour that the water in Regent Street was nearly two feet deep. Another eye-witness was photographer Fred Palmer (his studio was in Cromwell Street). Somehow he kept his camera dry and recorded the flood scenes for posterity.

11. WESTCOTT PLACE & BIRCH STREET

This postcard view was published by Tomkins and Barrett of Regent Street. A 1905 advertisement stated that the firm boasted a staggering 86,400 coloured postcards of Swindon, in one edition. They were offered for sale at 3½d. for a packet of six, or two packets for 6d. In all likelihood the Edwardian shopper could have walked into Tomkins and Barrett's premises and bought a postcard of practically every street in Swindon. Today such cards change hands for several pounds each.

12. WESTCOTT STREET - 1918

This Hooper postcard view records the celebrations in Westcott Street to commemorate the ending of World War I. It shows that a community spirit flourished, even in the humblest of terraced streets. Cynics would say that this spirit belongs to the past, but the Silver Jubilee of 1977, with its attendant street parties happily disproved this. Today there is no community living here at all. Westcott Street and much of the surrounding area has been swept away under the banner of progress.

13. BEATRICE STREET LAKE

In pre 1914 times the Lake was the destination of the annual life-boat procession. A lifeboat would arrive at the Swindon Town Station in Old Town. From there it would be drawn on a big wagon by six horses along Devizes Road, down Victoria Hill, through the town and finish up by being launched on Beatrice Street Lake. A collection would be made from the crowds lining the streets in aid of what was then the Lifeboat Institution. Sadly both Lake and Procession are now only memories of the past.

14. FARINGDON STREET - 1908

This photograph of Faringdon Street (now Road) following the great snowstorm of April 25th 1908, complete with snow covered tramcar ploughing its way through the white streets, lends credence to the belief that hard winters are a thing of the past. The sender of this postcard wrote 'This is a photo of last Saturday here ...' Often postcards of unusual events were produced for sale within days of being photographed.

15. REGENT STREET

The main shopping area of New Swindon. The Artillery Arms pub and the County Electric Pavillion, Swindon's first cinema, stand on the right hand side of the street. Opposite is 'The Spot', a sports goods shop that became a Swindon institution. Sadly, 'The Spot' closed its doors to customers for the last time in 1979.

16. TRAM CENTRE

The Tram Centre, Fleet Street, just before the First World War. Tram car and horse and cart manage to co-exist in a world of trailing skirts and wide brimmed bonnets.

17. WILLIAM STREET

A typical nineteenth century street, with its pub 'The Park Hotel' on one corner and its shop 'The Cambrian Cake Shop' on the other. The name 'Cambria' is a reference to the Welsh settlement of GWR workers who lived in nearby Cambria Place.

18. CRICKLADE ROAD

It is almost impossible to believe that Cricklade Road was once a place safe enough for young children to stand in and play with their friends without the slightest risk of instant extermination. In fact, just the place to while away those long hot seemingly endless, Edwardian summers.

19. RODBOURNE ROAD TRAM TERMINUS

A seldom photographed area of Swindon, Rodbourne Road was one of the four Tramway Termini, the others were located at The Centre, Gorse Hill and Old Town. Replaced by motor buses in 1929, the trams still evoke a great appeal; perhaps they symbolise the nostalgia for the 'good old days' more than most things. A tramway photograph is particularly appropriate in view of the recent 75th Anniversary of Swindon's Tramways.

20. VICTORIA ROAD

An example of a street named after Royalty. Albert Street runs parallel.

21. THE SANDS

Old street names, like old traditions, die hard, especially in the heart of the Wiltshire countryside. This 1908 view of Bath Road is entitled 'The Sands', preferring to use the old 19th century name to the more imposing title officially bestowed in 1904.

22. RAILWAY VILLAGE - 1979

An excellent conservation programme by Thamesdown Council has restored the GWR village to its original exterior condition. It is important to remember that in the 1840s this village of 300 terraced houses WAS New Swindon - a self-contained community, paternally administered by the all-powerful railway company: a conception years ahead of its time.

23. GWR 'CASTLE' CLASS

GWR No 4087 Cardigan Castle. See Cardigan Close, The Lawn.

24. GWR 'HALL' CLASS

GWR No 5963 Wimpole Hall. See Wimpole Close, Park South

25. GWR STATION

The GWR Station at Swindon, photographed in the heyday of the 'golden age of steam'.

26. FLEET STREET

Fleet Street photographed just prior to the Great War. This photograph is taken from the large collection of glass plate negatives rescued from imminent destruction on a London building site. Rescued only just in time: this particular plate was already extensively damaged. Notice the boy with his hoop and stick in the foreground. This animated scene also reminds us of 'Budgetts Tea Stores', 'The Kings Head' and, in the background, 'Miles Drug Stores'. Maybe older readers will remember them?

27. WESLEY CHURCH, FARINGDON STREET

This building has had a chequered career. Originally erected by the GWR to house the influx of Welsh workers to the Rolling Mills in the 1860s, (see Cambria Place) and known as 'The Barracks', it later became a Wesleyan Methodist Church. Today the building houses the Town's Railway Museum - a part of Old Swindon that, thankfully, has escaped demolition.

28. REGENT CIRCUS

The Head Post Office and Picture House stand in an area of Swindon that was originally intended to be known as 'Trafalgar Square'. Perhaps the thought of additional stone lions was too much for our forefathers! Anyway they eventually settled for the less imposing title, 'Regent Circus'. The Picture House carries an advertisement for 'Vitagraph'. I wonder if this was an early trade name for a type of film, similar to our modern day 'Technicolour' and 'Cinemascope'? The advertisement illustrates a programme entitled 'The Artists Great Madonna' shown "in two parts".

29. RODBOURNE ROAD

Rodbourne Road in Edwardian days. These years are remembered by us in the troubled times of the 1970s as a golden era of peacefulness coupled with a leisurely tranquility reflected in seemingly endless hot summers. An age of straw boaters, long skirts and gentlemen sportsmen, exemplified by giants such as C B Fry and F S Jackson. It was also an age that knew poverty and disease and no organised welfare state; an era where old age often implied an existance in the workhouse.

30. THE MALL

The Mall was built in 1906 to house the prosperous Edwardian middle classes. The intervening years have little altered the appearance or character of this impressive roadway.

Photographs 5, 6, 7, 8 and 9 are prints selected from a collection of nearly 400 glass plate negatives of Swindon and Bristol street scenes found stacked in boxes on a building site in West London, and now in the possession of the author.

The plates, used for commercial postcards, were taken in 1913 by the Swindon photographer Fred Viner, who had a studio at 23 Fleet Street and were published by Tomkins and Barrett of 41 Regent Street.

Many of the plates show outstanding detail and provide a superb pictorial record of pre World War I Swindon and Bristol. The original postcards made from the plates are scarce and much sought after by collectors.

1

The Planks, Swindon.

2

3

4

5

Broad St. & St Luke's Church Swindon. 468.

6

7

8

9

10

11

12

74

The Lake, Beatrice Street, Swindon.   Protheroe & Simons, Swindon.

13

14

Regent Street, Swindon.

15

Tram Centre, Swindon.

16

William Street. Swindon.

17

NORTH CRESCENT, CRICKLADE R? SWINDON.

18

19

20

21

22

23

24

25

26

27

28

29

The Mall .Swindon.
451.

30

Viscount Emlyn

Joseph Armstrong

George Jackson
Churchward

Marquess of Salisbury

Sir Daniel Gooch

Harold Fleming

Levi Lapper Morse

Richard Jefferies

Isambard Kingdom Brunel

William IV

Queen Victoria

Queen Alexandra

Alfred, Lord Tennyson

Lord Kitchener

William Ewart Gladstone

Sir Francis Drake

Sir Walter Raleigh

William Dean

Sir Henry Bessemer

5.
Pinehurst: The First Planned Estate

Pinehurst was Swindon's first major estate development this century, being laid out from the 1920s onwards. Roads here, and on the later estate to the east, are named after British trees.

ACACIA GROVE	1933	MYRTLE GARDENS	1936
ASH GROVE	1933	OAK TREE AVENUE	1931
BEECH AVENUE	1925	PINEHURST ROAD	1924
CEDARS CLOSE	1947	PINETREE RISE	1968
CHERRY TREE GROVE	1933	POPLAR AVENUE	1933
CHESTNUT AVENUE	1927	ROWAN ROAD	1969
CYPRESS GROVE	1947	SYCAMORE GROVE	1938
ELM ROAD	1947	THE CIRCLE	1924
FIR TREE CLOSE	1972	TULIP TREE CLOSE	1974
HAWTHORN AVENUE	1933	WILLOWS AVENUE	1931
HAZEL GROVE	1927		
HOLLY CLOSE	1947		
HURST CRESCENT	1924		
LABURNUM ROAD	1927		
*LARCHMORE CLOSE	1976		
LIMES AVENUE	1924		
LINDEN AVENUE	1924		
MAPLE GROVE	1936		
MULBERRY GROVE	1947	* On the Greenmeadow Estate; originally planned as Beaulieu Close

6.
Old Walcot

Separated from the later estate at Walcot East by Queen's Drive. Road names are derived from Cotswold towns and villages.

ALVESCOT ROAD	1937
BAMPTON GROVE	1936
BIBURY ROAD	1938
BURFORD AVENUE	1938
CAMPDEN ROAD	1939
LANGFORD GROVE	1936
NORTON GROVE	1936
SHIPTON GROVE	1937

The Whale Bridge Mural
(Depicting the Golden Lion Bridge)

7.
Rodbourne Cheney

Built just after the Second World War, the roads south of Beech Avenue are named after wartime leaders.

ALANBROOKE CRESCENT

1947 - Alan Francis Brooke, 1st Viscount Alanbrooke was Commander-in-Chief of the home forces.

CUNNINGHAM ROAD

1947 - Sir Alan Cunningham was an Army officer who did much notable work in East Africa.

MONTGOMERY AVENUE

1947 - After Field Marshall Bernard Montgomery, 1st Viscount Alamein.

PORTAL ROAD

1947 - Charles, 1st Viscount Portal of Hungerford was an Air Vice-Marshall during the second World War.

POUND LANE

1947 - Sir Alfred Dudley Pound was Admiral of the Fleet.

TEDDER CLOSE

1947 - After the Air Vice Marshall, Arthur Tedder.

TOVEY ROAD

1947 - John Cronin, 1st Baron Tovey, was an Admiral in the Royal Navy.

WAVELL ROAD

1947 - Archibald, 1st Earl Wavell, was a General during the war and later became Viceroy of India.

WINGATE PARADE

1959 - After Sir Reginald, 1st Baronet Wingate, General and Governor of the Sudan.

8.
The New Era: Post-War Estates

The first two decades of this Century saw only sporadic growth. Several estates - both private and council - sprung up during the 20s and 30s, though it was not until 1952 that the second chapter of expansion in Swindon's history really began. This was the year when the Council decided that Swindon should become an expanding town under the Town Development Act. The level of activity at the railway works had fallen off sharply since the war and the Council at last realised the danger to the town's prosperity if continued reliance were put on the Works for employment. New industries were attracted to the town, mainly from London, and this led to the construction of the modern industrial estates which are such a prominent feature of the town today.

Nowadays, few new roads are being built within the old Borough of Swindon as most of the town's expansion is taking place beyond the former boundaries. The Director of Technical Services at the Borough of Thamesdown is authorised to name new roads, after consultation with the Post Office and other interested parties. In practice, names are still often put forward by the developers themselves.

Penhill

The theme on this estate is Wiltshire Villages

ALDBOURNE CLOSE	1953	INGLESHAM ROAD	1952
ALLINGTON ROAD	1953	LACOCK ROAD	1951
ALTON CLOSE	1953	LATTON CLOSE	1954
AMESBURY CLOSE	1953	LEIGH ROAD	1954
ANSTY WALK	1954	LONGLEAT GARDENS	1964
ATWORTH CLOSE	1954	LYNEHAM CLOSE	1953
AVEBURY ROAD	1953	MARSTON AVENUE	1951
BERWICK WAY	1954	MELKSHAM CLOSE	1954
BRATTON CLOSE	1953	MILDENHALL WAY	1954
BREMHILL CLOSE	1952	MILSTON AVENUE	1952
BURBAGE ROAD	1953	MINETY ROAD	1954
CHARLTON CLOSE	1951	NEWTON WAY	1954
CHIPPENHAM CLOSE	1974	OAKSEY ROAD	1952
CHIPPENHAM WALK	1954	ODSTOCK ROAD	1953
CORSHAM ROAD	1951	PATNEY WALK	1954
CRUDWELL WAY	1953	*PENHILL DRIVE	1951
DOWNTON ROAD	1953	PEWSHAM ROAD	1951
DURNFORD ROAD	1951	POTTERDOWN ROAD	1970
DURRINGTON WALK	1952	RAMSBURY AVENUE	1953
ENFORD AVENUE	1953	REDLYNCH CLOSE	1953
ERLESTOKE WAY	1953	RUSHALL CLOSE	1953
EVERLEIGH ROAD	1951	SEMLEY WALK	1954
FYFIELD AVENUE	1951	SHALBOURNE CLOSE	1953
GRAFTON ROAD	1951	SHERSTON AVENUE	1951
HANNINGTON CLOSE	1955	SHREWTON WALK	1953
HEDDINGTON CLOSE	1952	SOMERFORD CLOSE	1952
HEYWOOD CLOSE	1953	SOUTHWICK AVENUE	1953
HILMARTON AVENUE	1953	STAPLEFORD CLOSE	1974
IMBER WALK	1954	STAPLEFORD WAY	1954

STAVERTON WAY	1953	WESTWOOD ROAD	1953
STOCKTON ROAD	1954	WILCOT AVENUE	1951
TILSHEAD WALK	1954	WILTON WALK	1953
TISBURY CLOSE	1953	WINGFIELD AVENUE	1953
TOCKENHAM WAY	1953	WINSLEY CLOSE	1952
URCHFONT WAY	1954	WINTERSLOW ROAD	1953
WARMINSTER AVENUE	1953	WOODFORD CLOSE	1953
WESTBURY ROAD	1954		

* See section 4 for further details

The Lawns

Built on the fields of Park Farm and Church Farm, formerly part of
the Goddard estate - the family lived at The Lawn whence the name
of this estate is derived. The earlier roads bear the names of GWR
'Castle' class engines, while the slightly later developments to the
east of Windsor Road have the more general theme of stately homes
and historic cities.

ARUNDEL CLOSE	1963	
BALMORAL CLOSE	1958	
BANBURY CLOSE	1956 - GWR 'Castle' class engine No 7011 - 'Banbury Castle'	
BERKELEY LAWNS	1956 - GWR No 4085 - 'Berkeley Castle'	
BEVERSTONE GROVE	1957 - GWR No 5068 - 'Beverston Castle' - note mis-spelling	
BRAEMAR CLOSE	1962	
BRECON CLOSE	1954 - GWR No 5023 - 'Brecon Castle'	
BROUGHTON GRANGE	1976 - GWR No 5033 - 'Broughton Castle'	
BUCKINGHAM ROAD	1960	
CAERNARVON WALK	1961 - Originally planned as Belvedere Walk	
CAMBRIDGE CLOSE	1961	
CANTERBURY CLOSE	1962	
CARDIGAN CLOSE	1957 - GWR No 4087 - 'Cardigan Castle'	
*CLEEVE LAWNS	1956 - GWR No 5091 - 'Cleeve Abbey'	
DENBIGH CLOSE	1957 - GWR No 7032 - 'Denbigh Castle'	
DONNINGTON GROVE	1957 - GWR No 4089 - 'Donnington Castle'	
DORCHESTER ROAD	1957 - GWR No 4090 - 'Dorchester Castle'	
DUNRAVEN CLOSE	1957 - GWR No 5044 - 'Earl of Dunraven'	
DUNSTER CLOSE	1954 - GWR No 4093 - 'Dunster Castle'	
FARLEIGH CRESCENT	1956 - GWR No 5027 - 'Farleigh Castle'	
GUILDFORD AVENUE	1961	
HEREFORD LAWNS	1956 - GWR No 7022 - 'Hereford Castle'	
HIGHCLERE AVENUE	1957 - GWR No 4096 - 'Highclere Castle'	

```
KENILWORTH LAWNS   1956 - GWR No 4097 - 'Kenilworth Castle'
LUDLOW CLOSE       1957 - GWR No 5003 - Ludlow Castle
MELBOURNE CLOSE    1961
RAGLAN CLOSE       1954 - GWR No 5008 - 'Raglan Castle'
SANDRINGHAM ROAD   1958
TENBY CLOSE        1962 - GWR No 7026 - 'Tenby Castle'
WARDOUR CLOSE      1956 - GWR No 5066 - 'Wardour Castle'
WIGMORE AVENUE     1957 - GWR No 5022 - 'Wigmore Castle'
WINDSOR ROAD       1954 - GWR No 4082 - 'Windsor Castle'
```

* Spelt 'Cleve' until 1961 when the mistake was rectified

G.W.R. 'North Star'

Park North

The very general theme of English villages and towns has been adopted for the names here.

AXBRIDGE CLOSE	1959	- Somerset village
BANWELL AVENUE	1958	- Village in Avon
BARNSTAPLE CLOSE	1958	- Devonshire town
*BEAUFORT GREEN	1963	- After Henry Somerset, Duke of Beaufort
BEMBRIDGE CLOSE	1961	- Town on the Isle of Wight
*BENTLEY CLOSE	1957	- After Richard Bentley, scholar and critic
BIDEFORD CLOSE	1958	- Devonshire town
BISLEY CLOSE	1958	- Gloucestershire village
BODMIN CLOSE	1971	- Town in Cornwall
BRENDON WALK	1962	- Village in Devon
BRIDPORT ROAD	1960	- Town in Dorset
BRUTON WALK	1960	- Town in Somerset
BUCKLAND CLOSE	1957	- Oxfordshire village
BURNHAM ROAD	1958	- Buckinghamshire town
(CHERBURY WALK	1956	- See under Walcot East)
CHICKERELL ROAD	1958	- Dorset village
CLANFIELD ROAD	1960	- Oxfordshire village
CLEVEDON CLOSE	1957	- Resort in Avon
COWLEY WALK	1961	- Oxfordshire village
(DACRE ROAD	1956	- See under Walcot East)
DAWLISH ROAD	1960	- South Devon resort
DRAYCOTT CLOSE	1957	- Oxfordshire village
DULVERTON AVENUE	1957	- Village in Somerset
FAREHAM CLOSE	1958	- Town in Hampshire
GREENHAM WALK	1957	- Berkshire village
HARTLAND CLOSE	1961	- Devonshire village
HELSTON ROAD	1958	- Town in Cornwall
HONITON ROAD	1960	- Devonshire town

(HUNSDON CLOSE	1956	- See under Walcot East)
(HUNTLEY CLOSE	1957	- see under Walcot East)
KENTON CLOSE	1957	- Devonshire village
KINGSWOOD AVENUE	1957	- Gloucestershire village
LYNDHURST CRESCENT	1958	- Hampshire town
MIDHURST AVENUE	1960	- West Sussex town
OAKFORD WALK	1957	- Devonshire village
PENROSE WALK	1958	- Village in Cornwall
RADSTOCK AVENUE	1960	- Town in Avon
REDURTH CLOSE	1960	- Town in Cornwall
RINGWOOD CLOSE	1966	- Town in Hampshire
SHAFTESBURY AVENUE	1960	- Dorset town
SILVERTON ROAD	1960	- Devonshire village
TAVISTOCK ROAD	1960	- Devonshire town
TWYFORD CLOSE	1963	- Town in Berkshire
VERWOOD CLOSE	1960	- Dorset village
**WELCOMBE AVENUE	1957	- Devonshire village
WEYHILL CLOSE	1958	- Hampshire village
YEOVIL CLOSE	1960	- Town in Somerset

*Beaufort Green and Bentley Close are at Park North but their names fit in with the Walcot East theme of historical personalities.

**Welcombe Avenue was originally called Colebrook Avenue, after the nearby River Cole, but the name was soon changed to avoid confusion with Colebrook Road at Stratton.

Park South (i)

Roads have been named after engines of the Great Western 'Hall' class, built at Swindon from 1928 until 1950.

BERRINGTON ROAD	1957 - GWR 'Hall' class engine No 4912 - 'Berrington Hall'
BLAKESLEY CLOSE	1957 - GWR No 4909 - 'Blakesley Hall'
CAXTON CLOSE	1958 - GWR No 5922 - 'Caxton Hall'
CHARFIELD CLOSE	1957 - GWR No 6904 - 'Charfield Hall'
CHESFORD CLOSE	1957 - Probably GWR 'Grange' class No 6812 - 'Chesford Grange'
COLSTON CLOSE	1957 - GWR No 5923 - 'Colston Hall'
CRANMORE AVENUE	1957 - GWR No 4914 - 'Cranmore Hall'
CROSBY WALK	1957 - GWR No 4992 - 'Crosby Hall'
*CROSSWOOD ROAD	1957 - GWR No 4917 - 'Crosswood Hall'
DAVENHAM CLOSE	1957 - GWR No 6907 - 'Davenham Hall'
EATON CLOSE	1957 - GWR No 4921 - 'Eaton Hall'
ESHTON WALK	1957 - GWR No 6942 - 'Eshton Hall'
FARNBOROUGH ROAD	1957 - GWR No 4927 - 'Farnborough Hall'
GRANTLEY CLOSE	1957 - GWR No 6924 - 'Grantley Hall'
HANBURY ROAD	1956 - GWR No 4931 - 'Hanbury Hall'
HENLEY ROAD	1957 - GWR No 5983 - 'Henley Hall'
KELHAM CLOSE	1957 - GWR No 5904 - 'Kelham Hall'
KIMBERLEY ROAD	1956 - GWR No 6952 - 'Kimberley Hall'
KINGSWAY CLOSE	1957 - GWR No 5933 - 'Kingsway Hall'
KIRBY CLOSE	1960 - GWR No 5993 - 'Kirby Hall'
KNOLTON WALK	1957 - GWR No 5958 - 'Knolton Hall'
KNOWSLEY WALK	1956 - GWR No 5905 - 'Knowsley Hall'
LAWTON ROAD	1977 - GWR No 5906 - 'Lawton Hall'
LEIGHTON AVENUE	1957 - GWR No 6953 - 'Leighton Hall'
NORCLIFFE ROAD	1961 - GWR No 6957 - 'Norcliffe Hall'
OLDLANDS WALK	1960 - GWR No 6917 - 'Oldlands Hall'

PRIORY ROAD	1961 - GWR No 4958 - 'Priory Hall'
PURLEY AVENUE	1957 - GWR No 4959 - 'Purley Hall'
RIPON WAY	1957 - GWR No 5914 - 'Ripon Hall'
RODWELL CLOSE	1957 - GWR No 4964 - 'Rodwell Hall'
RUSHTON ROAD	1957 - GWR No 5913 - 'Rushton Hall'
STANWAY CLOSE	1957 - GWR No 4971 - 'Stanway Hall'
STEDHAM WALK	1962 - GWR No 6961 - 'Stedham Hall'
THORNBRIDGE ROAD	1957 - GWR No 6964 - 'Thornbridge Hall'
TRENTHAM CLOSE	1957 - GWR No 5915 - 'Trentham Hall'
TRINITY CLOSE	1977 - GWR No 5916 - 'Trinity Hall'
WALLSWORTH ROAD	1956 - GWR No 5974 - 'Wallsworth Hall'
WALTON CLOSE	1957 - GWR No 5918 - 'Walton Hall'
WARDLEY CLOSE	1957 - GWR No 5950 - 'Wardley Hall'
WHITBOURNE AVENUE	1957 - GWR No 5940 - 'Whitbourne Hall'
WIMPOLE CLOSE	1961 - GWR No 5963 - 'Wimpole Hall'
WOLSELY AVENUE	1957 - GWR No 5964 - 'Wolseley Hall' - note mis-spelling

* Residents have asked for the name to be changed; they believe the
fact that it has 13 letters is connected with the high number of
deaths in the road of late.

The Brunel Centre

Park South (ii)

The roads here are named after villages and towns in Britain.

AINSWORTH ROAD	1961 -	Lancashire village
AMERSHAM ROAD	1963 -	Town in Buckinghamshire
BELVEDERE ROAD	1961 -	East London suburb
CARSHALTON ROAD	1962 -	South London suburb
CARSTAIRS AVENUE	1962 -	Town in Strathclyde
CAVENDISH SQUARE	1961 -	Suffolk village
DALWOOD CLOSE	c1972 -	Devon village
DENHOLME ROAD	1961 -	West Yorkshire village
ECCLESTON CLOSE	1962 -	Lancashire village
HAZLEMERE CLOSE	1962 -	Lancashire village
HELMSDALE WALK	1961 -	Highland town
HILLINGDON ROAD	1961 -	West London suburb
HORHAM CRESCENT	1972 -	Shropshire village
KEMERTON WALK	1973 -	Worcestershire village
KESWICK ROAD	1962 -	Cumbrian town
KEYNSHAM WALK	1961 -	Town in Avon
KINGSTON ROAD	1961 -	Surrey town
LOXLEY WALK	1961 -	Warwickshire village
MERIDEN WALK	1961 -	West Midlands village
MONKTON CLOSE	1962 -	Wiltshire village
NETHERTON CLOSE	1962 -	Oxfordshire village
PAKENHAM ROAD	1962 -	Suffolk town
PARKSTONE WALK	1961 -	Dorset village
PETERSFIELD ROAD	1962 -	Hampshire town
ROSEDALE ROAD	1961 -	North Yorkshire village
ROYSTON ROAD	1961 -	Town in Hertfordshire
SHERWOOD ROAD	1964 -	Nottinghamshire village
STUDLAND CLOSE	1963 -	Dorset village
TAPLOW WALK	1961 -	Buckinghamshire town

Walcot East

The names here are derived from notable Britons of the 16th and 17th Centuries.

ASHLEY CLOSE	1956 - Anthony Ashley Cooper, 1st Earl of Shaftesbury
(BEAUFORT GREEN	1963 - See under Park North)
BEAUMONT ROAD	1957 - Francis Beaumont, a leading 17th Century dramatist
BEDFORD ROAD	1958 - John Russell, 1st Earl of Bedford, a prominent statesman. Known as Bedford Green unti 1961
(BENTLEY CLOSE	1957 - See under Park North)
BOTHWELL ROAD	1958 - James Hepburn, 4th Earl of Bothwell, was the third husband of Mary Queen of Scots
BROMLEY CLOSE	c1956 - Sir Thomas Bromley, lawyer and Lord Chancellor
BUCKHURST CRESCENT	1956 - Thomas Sackville, a statesman and dramatist, was created Lord Buckhurst in 1567
BURGHLEY CLOSE	1956 - William Cecil, 1st Baron Burghley, was chief minister to Elizabeth I
CALVERT ROAD	1956 - George Calvert, 1st Baron Baltimore
CECIL ROAD	1960 - See Burghley Close
COURTENAY ROAD	1956 - Sir William Courtenay, courtier to Henry VIII
*DACRE ROAD	1956 - After the Cumbrian village
DALTON ROAD	1956 - John Dalton, poet
DARNLEY CLOSE	1956 - Lord Henry Stuart Darnley, second husband of Mary Queen of Scots
DOUGLAS ROAD	c1956 - James Douglas, Regent of Scotland from 1572 - 1578

DRAKES WAY	1956 - Sir Francis Drake, the celebrated admiral
DRAYTON WALK	1958 - Michael Drayton, poet
DUDLEY ROAD	1956 - John Dudley, 1st Duke of Northumberland
ESSEX WALK	1956 - Robert Devereux, a famous soldier, was the 2nd Earl of Essex
FAIRFAX CLOSE	1958 - Thomas Fairfax, 3rd Baron Fairfax of Cameron, a Parliamentarian general during the Civil War
FROBISHER DRIVE	1956 - Sir Martin Frobisher, navigator and vice-admiral
GRESHAM CLOSE	1956 - Sir Thomas Gresham, founder of the Royal Exchange
HAMILTON CLOSE	1956 - James Hamilton, 2nd Earl of Arran
HATTON GROVE	1956 - Sir Christopher Hatton, courtier and Lord Chancellor. Originally named Hatton Close
HARRINGTON WALK	1956 - James Harrington, political philospher
HERTFORD CLOSE	1959 - Edward Seymour, 1st Earl of Hertford
HOLLAND WALK	1959
HOWARD CLOSE	1959 - Catherine Howard, Henry VIIIs 5th Queen
*HUNSDON CLOSE	1956 - After the Hertfordshire village
*HUNTLEY CLOSE	1957 - After the Gloucestershire village
LENNOX DRIVE	1956 - Margaret Douglas, Countess of Lennox
MAITLAND ROAD	1956 - William Maitland, secretary of state
MARKHAM CLOSE	1956 - Gervase Markham, poet
MARLOWE AVENUE	1956 - Christopher Marlowe, poet and dramatist
MASSINGER WALK	1958 - Phillip Massinger, Wiltshire-born playwright
MELVILLE CLOSE	1956 - Andrew Melville, Scottish Presbytarian leader
NAUNTON ROAD	1956 - Sir Robert Naunton, statesman and writer
NORFOLK CLOSE	1956 - Thomas Howard, 4th Duke of Norfolk
RALEIGH AVENUE	1956 - Sir Walter Raleigh, famous adventurer
RANDOLPH CLOSE	1956 - Sir Thomas Randolph, political agent and ambassador
ROGERS CLOSE	1956 - John Rogers, a Protestant martyr
RUSSELL WALK	1959 - See Bedford Green

SACKVILLE CLOSE	1956 - See Buckhurst Crescent
SADLER WALK	1956 - Sir Ralph Sadler, diplomatist
**SELDEN CLOSE	c1958 - John Selden, antiquarian and politician
SEYMOUR ROAD	c1957 - See Hertford Close
SHIRLEY CLOSE	1956 - James Shirley, poet and dramatist
SHREWSBURY ROAD	1956 - George Talbot, 6th Earl of Shrewsbury
***SIDNEY CLOSE	c1956 - Sir Philip Sidney, politician and author
SOMERVILLE ROAD	1956 - William Somerville, poet and writer
SPENSER CLOSE	1956 - Edmund Spenser, poet
STUART CLOSE	1956 - See Darnley Close
SUSSEX SQUARE	1957 - Sir Thomas Radcliffee, 3rd Earl of Sussex
TUDOR WALK	1956 - Mary Tudor, Queen of France and Duchess of Suffolk
WALSINGHAM ROAD	1956 - Sir Francis Walsingham, secretary to Queen Elizabeth I

*Cherbury Walk, Dacre Road, Hunsdon Close and Huntley Close are all at Walcot East, but their names fit in with the theme of English villages at Park North.

**Selden Close is the access road to Derby Court, at present un-signposted.

***Sidney Close no longer exists. Originally an access road between Bromley Road and Holland Walk, it has now been grassed over.

The Oasis

Greenmeadow

Twenty-one of the roads on this estate are named after English rivers; eight of these fall within the old Borough of Swindon.

DART AVENUE	1961	
ISIS CLOSE	1961	
KENNET AVENUE	1961	(Originally Kennet Close)
SEVERN AVENUE	1962	
*STOUR WALK	1961	
TAMAR CLOSE	1961	
THAMES AVENUE	1961	
WINDRUSH AVENUE	1961	

* Changed to Stour Road in 1970, then back to Stour Walk in 1974

APPENDIX I - 'THE ROADWAY IN WAR'

The men such as Crombey and Whitehead who built Swindon's Roadways
envisaged a peaceful existence for both their buildings and the people
that lived in them. Hitler's Luftwaffe, however, had other ideas.

On the night of Sunday 20th October 1940 two heavy high explosive bombs
were dropped on Swindon, or as the Evening Advertiser reported evasively,
"a town in the south". The bombs fell on Rosebery and Graham Streets
and York Road, destroying many houses and killing ten people. The
'Advertiser' recounted the details in chilling prose. "In one street,
six ad-joining houses collapsed when a heavy bomb crashed through the
roof of one and left a crater marking the site where the house stood.
The second bomb dropped in the middle of a road in an adjoining street,
leaving another huge crater and almost completely demolishing three
houses". The newspaper added, "Demolition and rescue squads were quickly
at hand extricating residents trapped deep down in the wreckage and
attending to the injured".

Tragically, as in all conflicts, people are the prime sufferers. Ten
Swindonians were killed by the bombs, including an unidentified young
couple who were found dead in one street. However, the stories of the
survivors made for more optimistic reading. Two young girls were rescued
unharmed from beneath a completely wrecked house. One asked for a drink
and when offered a flask of water observed with a smile, 'Is that the best
you can do?'

A warden who entered one damaged house found an elderly couple fast asleep
in blankets, apparently unaware that there had been a raid. A tragi-comic
touch was provided by a newspaper boy who posted papers through the letter
box of a door that had been torn away from its hinges and was lying in the
passage of a half-demolished house. Included among those who had narrow
escapes was a woman, who after experiencing several weeks of bombing in a
northern town, had come south for a rest. In another home which was badly
damaged were two brothers, members of the fighting forces who had come
home the previous day on leave. Neither was injured.

'Generally' the Advertiser concluded "the inhabitants displayed great
fortitude and calmness". It was as well that they did, for the Rosebery
Street raid was merely the beginning of a succession of raids that brought
death and destruction to Swindon's streets:

19th December 1940 - 10 bombs fell on Beatrice Street and Kembrey Street -
                     1 killed.
17th August   1942 - bombs dropped on Ferndale Road and Kembrey Street -
                     25 killed.
29th August   1942 - bombs dropped on Drove Road - 8 killed and 300 houses
                     damaged.

In total the Luftwaffe dropped 104 bombs on the Swindon district, killing 48
people, destroying 50 houses and damaging 1,852. Despite the suffering and
hardship endured by the 'Roadway in War', British resistance and good humour
was typified by the young newspaper boy who showed that life still goes on.
Such an attitude carried us through to ultimate victory in 1945.

Bibliography

Contemporary Biographies: Wilts & Dorset   Pike 1906

Documents Related to the Goddard Family of North Wiltshire
                                        Swindon Public Libraries

Great Western Engines, Numbers, Types & Classes
                                    Brian Whitehurst O.P.C. 1970

Jefferies' Land: A History of Swindon & its Environs
                                        Richard Jefferies 1896

Studies in the History of Swindon   Grinsell et al
                                    Swindon Borough Council 1950

Swindon Street Names   W.H. Hallam Wiltshire Archaeological & Natural
            History Society's Magazine, Vol 48 p 523 and Vol 49 p 487

The Place-Names of Wiltshire   Gover, Mawer & Stenton C.U.P. 1939

Victoria County History of Wiltshire Vol IX   O.U.P. 1970

Swindon 'Fifty Years Ago' - William Morris - Swindon Advertiser 1885
                                    Republished by Tabard Press 1970

A Swindon Retrospect   Frederick Large 1932   Replublished by
                                            S.R. Publishers 1970

Thanks

Caroline Ireland who did the line drawings

Eileen Roberts of the Borough of Thamesdown Technical Services Department

Wiltshire Library and Museum Service

Wiltshire Newspapers for the photograph of Harold Fleming

Wiltshire County Council Archives Department at Trowbridge

Mike Stone who did the portrait photographs

Fred Stevens and Nigel Bown who loaned postcards from their collections

John Rowe

Leslie Jones

And all the many other people who have helped us

"Roads go on
While we forget, and are
Forgotten like a star
That shoots and is gone"

'Roads' by Edward Thomas
(1878-1917)
Killed in action 1917

Murray John Building

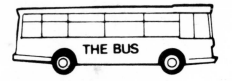